PENGUIN BOOKS

THE ESQUIRE BOOK OF SPORTS WRITING

Greg Williams was born and lives in north London. He has worked at *Esquire* since its UK launch in March 1991.

The Esquire Book of Sports Writing

Edited by Greg Williams

PENGUIN BOOKS

PENGUIN BOOKS

Published by the Penguin Group
Penguin Books Ltd, 27 Wrights Lane, London w8 5tz, England
Penguin Books USA Inc., 375 Hudson Street, New York, New York 10014, USA
Penguin Books Australia Ltd, Ringwood, Victoria, Australia
Penguin Books Canada Ltd, 10 Alcorn Avenue, Toronto, Ontario, Canada m4v 3b2
Penguin Books (NZ) Ltd, 182–190 Wairau Road, Auckland 10, New Zealand

Penguin Books Ltd, Registered Offices: Harmondsworth, Middlesex, England

Published in Penguin Books 1995
10 9 8 7 6 5 4 3 2 1

Set in 11/13.5pt Monophoto Bembo
Typeset by Datix International Limited, Bungay, Suffolk
Printed in England by Clays Ltd, St Ives plc

Contents

Acknowledgements

Thanks to Tim Hulse, David Hirshey and Eric Perrett, who all know their sport. And a special thank you to Rosie Boycott, editor of *Esquire*.

The pieces in this volume are reprinted by permission of the authors, unless otherwise stated. 'The Silent Season of a Hero' copyright © Gay Talese, 1966. 'Great Men Die Twice' copyright © Mark Kram, 1989. 'Michael Jordan Leaps the Great Divide' copyright © John Edgar Wideman, 1990; reprinted by permission of the author and Wylie, Aitken & Stone Inc. 'And Then He Kissed Me' copyright © Gordon Burn, 1990. 'The Shame of Argentina' copyright © Colm Tóibín, 1991. 'The Afterlife' copyright © Paul Morley, 1991. 'The Grudge Match', copyright © Martin Amis and Julian Barnes, 1991; reprinted by permission of the authors and Peters, Fraser & Dunlop Group Ltd. 'The Other Code' copyright © Thomas Keneally, 1991; reprinted by permission of the author and Tessa Sayle Agency. 'Hats Off to Don King' copyright © Mike Lupica, 1991. 'Ireland's War on Eamon Dunphy' copyright © Colm Tóibín, 1992. 'Becker' copyright © Gordon Burn, 1992. 'The Agony of Being a Fan' copyright © Nick Hornby, 1992. 'In Search of the Silver King' copyright © James Fox, 1992. 'Learning to Live in Me-shaped Space' copyright © Lawrence Norfolk, 1992. 'Jimmy White and his Magic Finger' copyright © Laura Thompson, 1993. 'Playing Handball with Zeus' (originally entitled 'Stairway to Heaven') copyright © Timothy O'Grady, 1993. 'The Education of Mike Tyson' copyright © Pete Hamill, 1994; reprinted by permission of the author and International Creative Management Inc.

Introduction

'The great fallacy is that the game is first and last about winning. It's nothing of the kind. The game is about glory. It's about doing things in style, with a flourish, about going out and beating the other lot, not waiting for them to die of boredom.' – Danny Blanchflower, former captain of Tottenham Hotspur.

My grandfather watched the great Spurs double-winning team from the Paxton Road end at White Hart Lane. The 1960–61 season was a time of glory. Captained by Danny Blanchflower, Tottenham rode roughshod over the rest of what was then called the First Division, garnering a reputation as a free-spirited, mercurial team whose style was centred on attack. My grandfather thought that this was the way the game should be played. For him Spurs were a collusion of wizardry and spontaneity, of the robust and the divine. I think it came as a great disappointment to him when, aged six, I decided to worship at the unsanctified ground two miles down the Seven Sisters Road.

In the following collection I hope that some of the ingenuity and boldness of that Tottenham side is apparent. Just as Blanchflower's side approached the game in a novel way, the kind of writing published in *Esquire* seeks to negotiate the familiar in a fresh and original way; it is the manner in which

Esquire writers approach stories that has given the magazine its reputation for quality non-fiction writing. The likes of George Best and Mike Tyson have been written about countless times, but what *Esquire* attempts to provide is the definitive piece, the final word.

Since the Victorian era sport has been a touchstone for people in pubs, shops and offices around the country. Although the 1860s witnessed the setting up of the English Football Association, golf's first open tournament, England's first athletics championship and the first England cricket tour of Australia, it took another century before the birth of a literary movement that treated sport with the level of seriousness with which it was popularly regarded. Although realism was introduced into English literature in the eighteenth century, it was only thirty years ago that feature writers began to use the techniques of non-fiction writing to elevate their work above hackery.

The advent of what was to become known as the new journalism proved a boon for American sports writers in the early 1960s. A new generation of reporters whose brief it was to delve deep below the surface of the sports events were let loose to bring the reader the smell of the dressing room and the crunch of the tackle. So it was in 1963 that George Plimpton spent months with the Detroit Lions football team in order to produce his masterful *Paper Lion*, one of the wisest, most observant books ever written about sport.

Sport suddenly seemed to be a method of revealing something about the times, something that was prescient and tapped into the culture through subject matter that was tangible and unsophisticated yet elicited passion and involved the reader so that he or she would be absorbed in the same way they would if reading a novel.

In this country these techniques were adopted by many in journalism, most notably by Hugh McIlvanney in his writing for the *Observer*. Yet for years sport and literature were barely on speaking terms. That's all changed. Nick Hornby's *Fever Pitch* demonstrated that it's possible to write on sport in a way that is personal yet universal. Although ostensibly a memoir about an obsession with one club, the book struck a chord with a broad constituency of fans so long perceived as feeble-witted and outside the province of publishers, who are rarely drawn from the ranks of the football-watching classes.

This collection suggests that publishers are making up for their neglect of sports writing. We've selected a range of pieces that span writing from the first wave of new journalism – Gay Talese's 'The Silent Season of a Hero' about Joe DiMaggio – right up to Pete Hamill's encounter with Mike Tyson at the Indiana Youth Center in 'The Education of Mike Tyson'. The collection is bound together by little more than the virtue of the pieces being commissioned by editors at *Esquire* here or in the US. Purists may baulk at the broad interpretation of sport which means that pieces about parachuting and fishing have been included. It's arguable that 'proper' sport is about competition, about beating opponents and winning trophies. But the pieces mentioned above demonstrate that there is a type of experiential writing about outdoor pursuits in the first person that may be considered akin to sports writing.

In our opinion this collection represents the best sports writing published in British *Esquire* during the four years of its existence. As far as US *Esquire* is concerned, its long and distinguished history means that this is just a taste of the best writing; we've had to be selective. In its sixty-odd-year history there's been so much sports writing that it would have been possible to publish a book solely consisting of the best baseball writing, but this would probably have a limited constituency on this side of the Atlantic.

Inevitably the book is monopolized by the twin temples

that dominate the best writing about sport, namely football and boxing. The latter has always attracted the finest writers, because it is the most elemental of sports, demanding incredible skill and absolute bravery, the ring being the place where it is impossible to escape scrutiny, where man's instinct and brain must work in their closest harmony.

Football has never been blessed with writers to rival those of boxing, but because of its huge popularity occasionally a writer will step forward and lay bare a subject about which it seems there is little more to say. Such a piece is 'The Afterlife' by Paul Morley which was published in *Esquire* in 1991. It's an extraordinary piece of work, operating as much more than a profile of self-destructive genius, a story as emotionally involving as fiction, proving that sport, with its in-built drama and emotion, is about nothing less than life itself. I like to think that Danny Blanchflower would have approved.

Greg Williams, London, February 1995

The Silent Season of a Hero

GAY TALESE

> '"I would like to take the great DiMaggio fishing," the old man said. "They say his father was a fisherman. Maybe he was as poor as we are and would understand."' — Ernest Hemingway, *The Old Man and the Sea*

It was not quite spring, the silent season before the search for salmon, and the old fishermen of San Francisco were either painting their boats or repairing their nets along the pier or sitting in the sun talking quietly among themselves, watching the tourists come and go, and smiling, now, as a pretty girl paused to take their picture. She was about twenty-five, healthy and blue-eyed and wearing a red turtle-neck sweater, and she had long, flowing blonde hair that she brushed back a few times before clicking her camera. The fishermen, looking at her, made admiring comments but she did not understand because they spoke a Sicilian dialect; nor did she notice the tall grey-haired man in a dark suit who stood watching her from behind a big bay window on the second floor of DiMaggio's Restaurant that overlooks the pier.

He watched until she left, lost in the crowd of newly arrived tourists that had just come down the hill by cable car. Then he sat down again at the table in the restaurant, finishing his tea and lighting another cigarette, his fifth in the last half-hour. It was eleven-thirty in the morning. None of the other tables was occupied, and the only sounds came from the bar where a liquor salesman was laughing at something the headwaiter had said. But then the salesman, his briefcase under his arm, headed for the door, stopping briefly to peek into the dining room and call out, 'See you later, Joe.' Joe DiMaggio turned and waved at the salesman. Then the room was quiet again.

At fifty-one, DiMaggio was a most distinguished-looking man, aging as gracefully as he had played on the ball field, impeccable in his tailoring, his nails manicured, his six-foot two-inch body seeming as lean and capable as when he posed for the portrait that hangs in the restaurant and shows him in Yankee Stadium swinging from the heels at a pitch thrown twenty years ago. His grey hair was thinning at the crown, but just barely, and his face was lined in the right places, and his expression, once as sad and haunted as a matador's, was more in repose these days, though, as now, tension had returned and he chain-smoked and occasionally paced the floor and looked out the window at the people below. In the crowd was a man he did not wish to see.

The man had met DiMaggio in New York. This week he had come to San Francisco and had telephoned several times but none of the calls had been returned because DiMaggio suspected that the man, who had said he was doing research on some vague sociological project, really wanted to delve into DiMaggio's private life and that of DiMaggio's former wife, Marilyn Monroe. DiMaggio would never tolerate this. The memory of her death is still very painful to him, and yet, because he keeps it to himself, some people are not sensitive to it. One night in a supper club a woman who had been drinking approached his table, and when he did not ask her to join him, she snapped:

'All right, I guess I'm *not* Marilyn Monroe.'

He ignored her remark, but when she repeated it, he replied, barely controlling his anger, 'No – I wish you were, but you're not.'

The tone of his voice softened her, and she asked, 'Am I saying something wrong?'

'You already have,' he said. 'Now will you please leave me alone?'

His friends on the wharf, understanding him as they do, are very careful when discussing him with strangers, knowing that should they inadvertently betray a confidence he will not denounce them but rather will never speak to them again; this comes from a sense of propriety not inconsistent in the man who also, after Marilyn Monroe's death, directed that fresh flowers be placed on her grave 'forever'.

Some of the older fishermen who have known DiMaggio all his life remember him as a small boy who helped clean his father's boat, and as a young man who sneaked away and used a broken oar as a bat on the sandlots nearby. His father, a small mustachioed man known as Zio Pepe, would become infuriated and call him *lagnuso*, lazy, *meschino*, good-for-nothing, but in 1936 Zio Pepe was among those who cheered when Joe DiMaggio returned to San Francisco after his first season with the New York Yankees and was carried along the wharf on the shoulders of the fishermen.

The fishermen also remember how, after his retirement in 1951, DiMaggio brought his second wife, Marilyn, to live near the wharf, and sometimes they would be seen early in the morning fishing off DiMaggio's boat, the *Yankee Clipper*, now docked quietly in the marina, and in the evening they would be sitting and talking on the pier. They had arguments, too, the fishermen knew, and one night Marilyn was seen running hysterically, crying as she ran, along the road away from the pier, with Joe following. But the fishermen

3

pretended they did not see this; it was none of their affair.
They knew that Joe wanted her to stay in San Francisco and
avoid the sharks in Hollywood, but she was confused and
torn then – 'She was a child,' they said – and even today
DiMaggio loathes Los Angeles and many of the people in it.
He no longer speaks to his onetime friend, Frank Sinatra,
who had befriended Marilyn in her final years, and he also is
cool to Dean Martin and Peter Lawford and Lawford's former
wife, Pat, who once gave a party at which she introduced
Marilyn Monroe to Robert Kennedy, and the two of them
danced often that night, Joe heard, and he did not take it
well. He was very possessive of her that year, his close friends
say, because Marilyn and he had planned to remarry; but
before they could she was dead, and DiMaggio banned the
Lawfords and Sinatra and many Hollywood people from her
funeral. When Marilyn Monroe's attorney complained that
DiMaggio was keeping her friends away, DiMaggio answered
coldly, 'If it weren't for those friends persuading her to stay
in Hollywood she would still be alive.'

Joe DiMaggio now spends most of the year in San Francisco, and each day tourists, noticing the name on the restaurant, ask the men on the wharf if they ever see him. Oh yes,
the men say, they see him nearly every day; they have not
seen him yet this morning, they add, but he should be
arriving shortly. So the tourists continue to walk along the
piers past the crab vendors, under the circling sea gulls, past
the fish 'n' chip stands, sometimes stopping to watch a large
vessel steaming toward the Golden Gate Bridge which, to
their dismay, is painted red. Then they visit the Wax Museum,
where there is a life-size figure of DiMaggio in uniform, and
walk across the street and spend a quarter to peer through the
silver telescopes focused on the island of Alcatraz, which is no
longer a Federal prison. Then they return to ask the men if
DiMaggio has been seen. Not yet, the men say, although they

notice his blue Impala parked in the lot next to the restaurant. Sometimes tourists will walk into the restaurant and have lunch and will see him sitting calmly in a corner signing autographs and being extremely gracious with everyone. At other times, as on this particular morning when the man from New York chose to visit, DiMaggio was tense and suspicious.

When the man entered the restaurant from the side steps leading to the dining room he saw DiMaggio standing near the window talking with an elderly maître d' named Charles Friscia. Not wanting to walk in and risk intrusion, the man asked one of DiMaggio's nephews to inform Joe of his presence. When DiMaggio got the message he quickly turned and left Friscia and disappeared through an exit leading down to the kitchen.

Astonished and confused, the visitor stood in the hall. A moment later Friscia appeared and the man asked, 'Did Joe leave?'

'Joe who?' Friscia replied.

'Joe DiMaggio!'

'Haven't seen him,' Friscia said.

'You haven't *seen* him! He was standing right next to you a second ago!'

'It wasn't me,' Friscia said.

'You were standing next to him. I saw you. In the dining room.'

'You must be mistaken,' Friscia said, softly, seriously. 'It wasn't me.'

'You *must* be kidding,' the man said, angrily, turning and leaving the restaurant. Before he could get to his car, however, DiMaggio's nephew came running after him and said, 'Joe wants to see you.'

He returned expecting to see DiMaggio waiting for him. Instead he was handed a telephone. The voice was powerful and deep and so tense that the quick sentences ran together.

'*You are invading my rights, I did not ask you to come, I assume you have a lawyer, you must have a lawyer, get your lawyer!*'

'I came as a friend,' the man interrupted.

'That's beside the point,' DiMaggio said. 'I have my privacy, I do not want it violated, you'd better get a lawyer . . .' Then, pausing, DiMaggio asked, 'Is my nephew there?'

He was not.

'Then wait where you are.'

A moment later DiMaggio appeared, tall and red-faced, erect and beautifully dressed in his dark suit and white shirt with the grey silk tie and the gleaming silver cuff links. He moved with big steps toward the man and handed him an airmail envelope, unopened, that the man had written from New York.

'Here,' DiMaggio said. 'This is yours.'

Then DiMaggio sat down at a small table. He said nothing, just lit a cigarette and waited, legs crossed, his head held high and back so as to reveal the intricate construction of his nose, a fine sharp tip above the big nostrils and tiny bones built out from the bridge, a great nose.

'Look,' DiMaggio said, more calmly. 'I do not interfere with other people's lives. And I do not expect them to interfere with mine. There are things about my life, personal things, that I refuse to talk about. And even if you asked my brothers they would be unable to tell you about them because they do not know. There are things about me, so many things, that they simply do not know . . .'

'I don't want to cause trouble,' the man said. 'I think you're a great man, and . . .'

'I'm not great,' DiMaggio cut in. 'I'm not great,' he repeated, softly. 'I'm just a man trying to get along.'

Then DiMaggio, as if realizing that he was intruding upon his own privacy, abruptly stood up. He looked at his watch.

'I'm late,' he said, very formal again. 'I'm ten minutes late. *You're* making me late.'

The man left the restaurant. He crossed the street and wandered over to the pier, briefly watching the fishermen hauling their nets and talking in the sun, seeming very calm and contented. Then, after he had turned and was headed back toward the parking lot, a blue Impala stopped in front of him and Joe DiMaggio leaned out the window and asked, 'Do you have a car?' His voice was very gentle.

'Yes,' the man said.

'Oh,' DiMaggio said. 'I would have given you a ride.'

Joe DiMaggio was not born in San Francisco but in Martinez, a small fishing village twenty-five miles northeast of the Golden Gate. Zio Pepe had settled there after leaving Isola delle Femmine, an islet off Palermo where the DiMaggios had been fishermen for generations. But in 1915, hearing of the luckier waters off San Francisco's wharf, Zio Pepe left Martinez, packing his boat with furniture and family, including Joe who was one year old.

San Francisco was placid and picturesque when the DiMaggios arrived, but there was a competitive undercurrent and struggle for power along the pier. At dawn the boats would sail out to where the bay meets the ocean and the sea is rough, and later the men would race back with their hauls, hoping to beat their fellow fishermen to shore and sell it while they could. Twenty or thirty boats would sometimes be trying to gain the channel shoreward at the same time, and a fisherman had to know every rock in the water, and later know every bargaining trick along the shore, because the dealers and restaurateurs would play one fisherman off against the other, keeping the prices down. Later the fishermen became wiser and organized, predetermining the maximum amount each fisherman would catch, but there were always some men who, like the fish, never learned, and so heads would sometimes be broken, nets slashed, gasoline poured on to their fish, flowers of warning placed outside their doors.

7

But these days were ending when Zio Pepe arrived, and he expected his five sons to succeed him as fishermen, and the first two, Tom and Michael, did; but a third, Vincent, wanted to sing. He sang with such magnificent power as a young man that he came to the attention of the great banker, A. P. Giannini, and there were plans to send him to Italy for tutoring and the opera. But there was hesitation around the DiMaggio household and Vince never went; instead he played ball with the San Francisco Seals and sportswriters misspelled his name.

It was DeMaggio until Joe, at Vince's recommendation, joined the team and became a sensation, being followed later by the youngest brother, Dominic, who was also outstanding. All three later played in the big leagues and some writers like to say that Joe was the best hitter, Dom the best fielder, Vince the best singer, and Casey Stengel once said: 'Vince is the only player I ever saw who could strike out three times in one game and not be embarrassed. He'd walk into the club-house whistling. Everybody would be feeling sorry for him, but Vince always thought he was doing good.'

After he retired from baseball Vince became a bartender, then a milkman, now a carpenter. He lives forty miles north of San Francisco in a house he partly built, has been happily married for thirty-four years, has four grandchildren, has in the closet one of Joe's tailor-made suits that he has never had altered to fit, and when people ask if he envies Joe he always says, 'No, maybe Joe would like to have what I have. He won't admit it, but he just might like to have what I have.' The brother Vince most admired was Michael, 'a big earthy man, a dreamer, a fisherman who wanted things but didn't want to take from Joe, or to work in the restaurant. He wanted a bigger boat, but wanted to earn it on his own. He never got it.' In 1953, at the age of forty-four, Michael fell from his boat and drowned.

Since Zio Pepe's death at seventy-seven in 1949, Tom, at sixty-two the oldest brother – two of his four sisters are older – has become nominal head of the family and manages the restaurant that was opened in 1937 as Joe DiMaggio's Grotto. Later Joe sold out his share and now Tom is co-owner of it with Dominic. Of all the brothers, Dominic, who was known as the 'Little Professor' when he played with the Boston Red Sox, is the most successful in business. He lives in a fashionable Boston suburb with his wife and three children and is president of a firm that manufactures fibre-cushion materials and grossed more than $3,500,000 last year.

Joe DiMaggio lives with his widowed sister, Marie, in a tan stone house on a quiet residential street not far from Fisherman's Wharf. He bought the house almost thirty years ago for his parents, and after their death he lived there with Marilyn Monroe; now it is cared for by Marie, a slim and handsome dark-eyed woman who has an apartment on the second floor, Joe on the third. There are some baseball trophies and plaques in the small room off DiMaggio's bedroom, and on his dresser are photographs of Marilyn Monroe, and in the living room downstairs is a small painting of her that DiMaggio likes very much: it reveals only her face and shoulders and she is wearing a very wide-brimmed sun hat, and there is a soft sweet smile on her lips, an innocent curiosity about her that is the way he saw her and the way he wanted her to be seen by others – a simple girl, 'a warm big-hearted girl,' he once described her, 'that everybody took advantage of'.

The publicity photographs emphasizing her sex appeal often offended him, and a memorable moment for Billy Wilder, who directed her in *The Seven Year Itch*, occurred when he spotted DiMaggio in a large crowd of people gathered on Lexington Avenue in New York to watch a scene in which Marilyn, standing over a subway grating to cool herself, had her skirts blown high by a sudden wind below. 'What the hell is going on here?' DiMaggio was overheard to have said in the crowd, and Wilder recalled, 'I shall never forget the look of death on Joe's face.'

He was then thirty-nine, she was twenty-seven. They had been married in January of that year, 1954, despite disharmony in temperament and time: he was tired of publicity, she was thriving on it; he was intolerant of tardiness, she was always late. During their honeymoon in Tokyo an American general had introduced himself and asked if, as a patriotic gesture, she would visit the troops in Korea. She looked at Joe. 'It's your honeymoon,' he said, shrugging, 'go ahead if you want to.'

She appeared on ten occasions before 100,000 servicemen, and when she returned she said, 'It was so wonderful, Joe. You never heard such cheering.'

'Yes I have,' he said.

Across from her portrait in the living room, on a coffee table in front of a sofa, is a sterling-silver humidor that was presented to him by his Yankee teammates at a time when he was the most talked-about man in America, and when Les Brown's band had recorded a hit that was heard day and night on the radio:

> . . . *From Coast to Coast, that's all you hear*
> *Of Joe the One-Man Show*
> *He's glorified the horsehide sphere,*
> *Jolting Joe DiMaggio . . .*
> *Joe . . . Joe . . . DiMaggio . . . we*
> *want you on our side . . .*

The year was 1941, and it began for DiMaggio in the middle of May after the Yankees had lost four games in a row, seven of their last nine, and were in fourth place, five-and-a-half games behind the leading Cleveland Indians. On May 15,

DiMaggio hit only a first-inning single in a game that New York lost to Chicago, 13–1; he was barely hitting .300, and had greatly disappointed the crowds that had seen him finish with a .352 average the year before and .381 in 1939.

He got a hit in the next game, and the next, and the next. On May 24, with the Yankees losing 6–5 to Boston, DiMaggio came up with runners on second and third and singled them home, winning the game, extending his streak to ten games. But it went largely unnoticed. Even DiMaggio was not conscious of it until it had reached twenty-nine games in mid-June. Then the newspapers began to dramatize it, the public became aroused, they sent him good-luck charms of every description, and DiMaggio kept hitting, and radio announcers would interrupt programmes to announce the news, and then the song again: '*Joe . . . Joe . . . DiMaggio . . . we want you on our side . . .*'

Sometimes DiMaggio would be hitless his first three times up, the tension would build, it would appear that the game would end without his getting another chance – but he always would, and then he would hit the ball against the left-field wall, or through the pitcher's legs, or between two leaping infielders. In the forty-first game, the first of a double-header in Washington, DiMaggio tied an American League record that George Sisler had set in 1922. But before the second game began a spectator sneaked on to the field and into the Yankees' dugout and stole DiMaggio's favourite bat. In the second game, using another of his bats, DiMaggio lined out twice and flied out. But in the seventh inning, borrowing one of his old bats that a teammate was using, he singled and broke Sisler's record, and he was only three games away from surpassing the major-league record of forty-four set in 1897 by Willie Keeler while playing for Baltimore when it was a National League franchise.

An appeal for the missing bat was made through the

newspapers. A man from Newark admitted the crime and returned it with regrets. And on July 2, at Yankee Stadium, DiMaggio hit a home run into the left-field stands. The record was broken.

He also got hits in the next eleven games, but on July 17 in Cleveland, at a night game attended by 67,468, he failed against two pitchers, Al Smith and Jim Bagby, Jr, although Cleveland's hero was really its third baseman, Ken Keltner, who in the first inning lunged to his right to make a spectacular back-handed stop of a drive and, from the foul line behind third base, he threw DiMaggio out. DiMaggio received a walk in the fourth inning. But in the seventh he again hit a hard shot at Keltner, who again stopped it and threw him out. DiMaggio hit sharply toward the shortstop in the eighth inning, the ball taking a bad hop, but Lou Boudreau speared it off his shoulder and threw to the second baseman to start a double play and DiMaggio's streak was stopped at fifty-six games. But the New York Yankees were on their way to winning the pennant by seventeen games, and the World Series too, and so in August, in a hotel suite in Washington, the players threw a surprise party for DiMaggio and toasted him with champagne and presented him with this Tiffany silver humidor that is now in San Francisco in his living room . . .

Marie was in the kitchen making toast and tea when DiMaggio came down for breakfast; his grey hair was uncombed but, since he wears it short, it was not untidy. He said goodmorning to Marie, sat down and yawned. He lit a cigarette. He wore a blue wool bathrobe over his pyjamas. It was eight a.m. He had many things to do today and he seemed cheerful. He had a conference with the president of Continental Television, Inc., a large retail chain in California of which he is a partner and vice-president; later he had a golf date, and then a big banquet to attend, and, if that did not go on too long and he were not too tired afterward, he might have a date.

Picking up the morning paper, not rushing to the sports page, DiMaggio read the front-page news, the people-problems of '66: Kwame Nkrumah was overthrown in Ghana, students were burning their draft cards (DiMaggio shook his head), the flu epidemic was spreading through the whole state of California. Then he flipped inside through the gossip columns, thankful they did not have him in there today – they had printed an item about his dating 'an electrifying airline hostess' not long ago, and they also spotted him at dinner with Dori Lane, 'the frantic frugger' in Whiskey à Go Go's glass cage – and then he turned to the sports page and read a story about how the injured Mickey Mantle may never regain his form.

It had all happened so quickly, the passing of Mantle, or so it seemed; he had succeeded DiMaggio as DiMaggio had succeeded Ruth, but now there was no great young power hitter coming up and the Yankee management, almost desperate, had talked Mantle out of retirement; and on September 18, 1965, they gave him a 'day' in New York during which he received several thousand dollars' worth of gifts – an automobile, two quarter horses, free vacation trips to Rome, Nassau, Puerto Rico – and DiMaggio had flown to New York to make the introduction before 50,000: it had been a dramatic day, an almost holy day for the believers who had jammed the grandstands early to witness the canonization of a new stadium saint. Cardinal Spellman was on the committee, President Johnson sent a telegram, the day was officially proclaimed by the Mayor of New York, an orchestra assembled in centre field in front of the trinity of monuments to Ruth, Gehrig, Huggins; and high in the grandstands, billowing in the breeze of early autumn, were white banners that read: 'Don't Quit Mick', 'We Love the Mick'.

The banners had been held by hundreds of young boys whose dreams had been fulfilled so often by Mantle, but also seated in the grandstands were older men, paunchy and balding, in whose middle-aged minds DiMaggio was still vivid and invincible, and some of them remembered how one month before, during a pre-game exhibition at Old-timers' Day in Yankee Stadium, DiMaggio had hit a pitch into the left-field seats, and suddenly thousands of people had jumped wildly to their feet, joyously screaming — the great DiMaggio had returned, they were young again, it was yesterday.

But on this sunny September day at the Stadium, the feast day of Mickey Mantle, DiMaggio was not wearing No. 5 on his back nor a black cap to cover his greying hair; he was wearing a black suit and white shirt and blue tie, and he stood in one corner of the Yankees' dugout waiting to be introduced by Red Barber, who was standing near home plate behind a silver microphone. In the outfield Guy Lombardo's Royal Canadians were playing soothing soft music; and moving slowly back and forth over the sprawling green grass between the left-field bull-pen and the infield were two carts driven by groundskeepers and containing dozens and dozens of large gifts for Mantle — a six-foot, one-hundred-pound Hebrew National salami, a Winchester rifle, a mink coat for Mrs Mantle, a set of Wilson golf clubs, a Mercury 95-horse-power outboard motor, a Necchi portable, a year's supply of Chunky candy. DiMaggio smoked a cigarette, but cupped it in his hands as if not wanting to be caught in the act by teen-aged boys near enough to peek down into the dugout. Then, edging forward a step, DiMaggio poked his head out and looked up. He could see nothing above except the packed towering green grandstands that seemed a mile high and moving, and he could see no clouds or blue sky, only a sky of faces. Then the announcer called out his name — '*Joe DiMaggio!*' — and suddenly there was a blast of cheering that grew louder and louder, echoing and reechoing within the big steel canyon, and DiMaggio stomped out his cigarette and climbed up the dugout steps and on to the soft green grass, the noise resounding in his ears, he could almost feel the breeze, the breath of 50,000 lungs upon him, 100,000 eyes watching every move and for the briefest instant as he walked he closed his eyes.

Then in his path he saw Mickey Mantle's mother, a smiling elderly woman wearing an orchid, and he gently reached out for her elbow, holding it as he led her toward the microphone next to the other dignitaries lined up on the infield. Then he stood, very erect and without expression, as the cheers softened and the Stadium settled down.

Mantle was still in the dugout, in uniform, standing with one leg on the top step, and lined on both sides of him were the other Yankees who, when the ceremony was over, would play the Detroit Tigers. Then into the dugout, smiling, came Senator Robert Kennedy, accompanied by two tall, curly-haired young assistants with blue eyes, Fordham freckles. Jim Farley was the first on the field to notice the Senator, and Farley muttered, loud enough for others to hear, 'Who the hell invited *him*?'

Toots Shor and some of the other committeemen standing near Farley looked into the dugout, and so did DiMaggio, his glance seeming cold, but he remaining silent. Kennedy walked up and down within the dugout shaking hands with the Yankees, but he did not walk on to the field.

'Senator,' said the Yankees' manager, Johnny Keane, 'why don't you sit down?' Kennedy quickly shook his head, smiled. He remained standing, and then one Yankee came over and asked about getting relatives out of Cuba, and Kennedy called over one of his aides to take down the details in a notebook.

On the infield the ceremony went on, Mantle's gifts continued to pile up – a Mobilette motor bike, a Sooner Schooner wagon barbecue, a year's supply of Chock Full O'Nuts coffee, a year's supply of Topps Chewing gum – and the Yankee players watched, and Maris seemed glum.

'Hey, Rog,' yelled a man with a tape recorder, Murray Olderman, 'I want to do a thirty-second tape with you.'

Maris swore angrily, shook his head.

'It'll only take a second,' Olderman said.

'Why don't you ask Richardson? He's a better talker than me.'

'Yes, but the fact that it comes from you . . .'

Maris swore again. But finally he went over and said in an interview that Mantle was the finest player of his era, a great competitor, a great hitter.

Fifteen minutes later, standing behind the microphone at home plate, DiMaggio was telling the crowd, 'I'm proud to introduce the man who succeeded me in centre field in 1951,' and from every corner of the Stadium the cheering, whistling, clapping came down. Mantle stepped forward. He stood with his wife and children, posed for the photographers kneeling in front. Then he thanked the crowd in a short speech, and, turning, shook hands with the dignitaries standing nearby. Among them now was Senator Kennedy, who had been spotted in the dugout five minutes before by Red Barber, and had been called out and introduced. Kennedy posed with Mantle for a photographer, then shook hands with the Mantle children, and with Toots Shor and James Farley and others. DiMaggio saw him coming down the line and at the last second he backed away, casually, hardly anybody noticing it, and Kennedy seemed not to notice it either, just swept past shaking more hands . . .

Finishing his tea, putting aside the newspaper, DiMaggio went upstairs to dress, and soon he was waving good-bye to Marie and driving toward his business appointment in downtown San Francisco with his partners in the retail television business. DiMaggio, while not a millionaire, has invested wisely and has always had, since his retirement from baseball, executive positions with big companies that have paid him well. He also was among the organizers of the Fisherman's National Bank of San Francisco last year, and, though it never came about, he demonstrated an acuteness that impressed those businessmen who had thought of him only in terms of baseball. He has had offers to manage big-league baseball teams but always has rejected them, saying, 'I have enough trouble taking care of my own problems without taking on the responsibilities of twenty-five ball-players.'

So his only contact with baseball these days, excluding public appearances, is his unsalaried job as a batting coach each spring in Florida with the New York Yankees, a trip he would make once again on the following Sunday, three days away, if he could accomplish what for him is always the dreaded responsibility of packing, a task made no easier by the fact that he lately has fallen into the habit of keeping his clothes in two places – some hang in his closet at home, some hang in the back room of a saloon called Reno's.

Reno's is a dimly-lit bar in the centre of San Francisco. A portrait of DiMaggio swinging a bat hangs on the wall, in addition to portraits of other star athletes, and the clientele consists mainly of the sporting crowd and newspapermen, people who know DiMaggio quite well and around whom he speaks freely on a number of subjects and relaxes as he can in few other places. The owner of the bar is Reno Barsocchini, a broadshouldered and handsome man of fifty-one with greying wavy hair who began as a fiddler in Dago Mary's tavern thirty-five years ago. He later became a bartender there and elsewhere, including DiMaggio's Restaurant, and now he is probably DiMaggio's closest friend. He was the best man at the DiMaggio–Monroe wedding in 1954, and when they separated nine months later in Los Angeles, Reno rushed down to help DiMaggio with the packing and drive him back to San Francisco. Reno will never forget the day.

Hundreds of people were gathered around the Beverly Hills home that DiMaggio and Marilyn had rented, and photographers were perched in the trees watching the windows, and others stood on the lawn and behind the rose bushes waiting to snap pictures of anybody who walked out of the house. The newspapers that day played all the puns – 'Joe Fanned on Jealousy'; 'Marilyn and Joe – Out at Home' – and the Hollywood columnists, to whom DiMaggio was never an idol, never a gracious host, recounted instances of incompatibility, and Oscar Levant said it all proved that no man could be a success in two national pastimes. When Reno Barsocchini arrived he had to push his way through the mob, then bang on the door for several minutes before being admitted. Marilyn Monroe was upstairs in bed, Joe DiMaggio was downstairs with his suitcases, tense and pale, his eyes bloodshot.

Reno took the suitcases and golf clubs out to DiMaggio's car, and then DiMaggio came out of the house, the reporters moving toward him, the lights flashing.

'Where are you going?' they yelled. 'I'm driving to San Francisco,' he said, walking quickly.

'Is that going to be your home?'

'That *is* my home and always has been.'

'Are you coming back?'

DiMaggio turned for a moment, looking up at the house.

'No,' he said, 'I'll never be back.'

Reno Barsocchini, except for a brief falling out over something he will not discuss, has been DiMaggio's trusted companion ever since, joining him whenever he can on the golf course or on the town, otherwise waiting for him in the bar with other middle-aged men. They may wait for hours sometimes, waiting and knowing that when he arrives he may wish to be alone; but it does not seem to matter, they are endlessly awed by him, moved by the mystique, he is a kind of male Garbo. They know that he can be warm and loyal if they are sensitive to his wishes, but they must never be late for an appointment to meet him. One man, unable to find a parking place, arrived a half-hour late once and DiMaggio did not talk to him again for three months. They know, too, when dining at night with DiMaggio, that he generally prefers male companions and occasionally one or two young women, but never wives; wives gossip, wives complain, wives are trouble, and men wishing to remain close to DiMaggio must keep their wives at home.

When DiMaggio strolls into Reno's bar the men wave and call out his name, and Reno Barsocchini smiles and announces, 'Here's the Clipper!' the 'Yankee Clipper' being a nickname from his baseball days.

'Hey, Clipper, Clipper,' Reno had said two nights before, 'where you been, Clipper? . . . Clipper, how 'bout a belt?'

DiMaggio refused the offer of a drink, ordering instead a pot of tea, which he prefers to all other beverages except before a date, when he will switch to vodka.

'Hey, Joe,' a sportswriter asked, a man researching a magazine piece on golf, 'why is it that a golfer, when he starts getting older, loses his putting touch first? Like Snead and Hogan, they can still hit a ball well off the tee, but on the greens they lose the strokes . . .'

'It's the pressure of age,' DiMaggio said, turning around on his bar stool. 'With age you get jittery. It's true of golfers, it's true of any man when he gets into his fifties. He doesn't take chances like he used to. The younger golfer, on the greens, he'll stroke his putts better. The older man, he becomes hesitant. A little uncertain. Shaky. When it comes to taking chances the younger man, even when driving a car, will take chances that the older man won't.'

'Speaking of chances,' another man said, one of the group that had gathered around DiMaggio, 'did you see that guy on crutches in here last night?'

'Yeah, had his leg in a cast,' a third said. 'Skiing.'

'I would never ski,' DiMaggio said. 'Men who ski must be doing it to impress a broad. You see these men, some of them forty, fifty, getting on to skis. And later you see them all bandaged up, broken legs . . .'

'But skiing's a very sexy sport, Joe. All the clothes, the tight pants, the fireplace in the ski lodge, the bear rug – Christ, nobody goes to ski. They just go out there to get it cold so they can warm it up . . .'

'Maybe you're right,' DiMaggio said. 'I might be persuaded.'

'Want a belt, Clipper?' Reno asked.

DiMaggio thought for a second, then said, 'All right – first belt tonight.'

Now it was noon, a warm sunny day. DiMaggio's business meeting with the television retailers had gone well; he had made a strong appeal to George Shahood, president of Continental Television, Inc., which has eight retail outlets in Northern California, to cut prices on colour television sets and increase the sales volume, and Shahood had conceded it was worth a try. Then DiMaggio called Reno's bar to see if there were any messages, and now he was in Lefty O'Doul's car being driven along Fisherman's Wharf toward the Golden Gate Bridge en route to a golf course thirty miles upstate. Lefty O'Doul was one of the great hitters in the National League in the early Thirties, and later he managed the San Francisco Seals when DiMaggio was the shining star. Though O'Doul is now sixty-nine, eighteen years older than DiMaggio, he nevertheless possesses great energy and spirit, is a hard-drinking, boisterous man with a big belly and roving eye; and when DiMaggio, as they drove along the highway toward the golf club, noticed a lovely blonde at the wheel of a car nearby and exclaimed, 'Look at *that* tomato!' O'Doul's head suddenly spun around, he took his eyes off the road, and yelled, 'Where, *where*?' O'Doul's golf game is less than what it was – he used to have a two-handicap – but he still shoots in the 80s, as does DiMaggio.

DiMaggio's drives range between 250 and 280 yards when he doesn't sky them, and his putting is good, but he is distracted by a bad back that both pains him and hinders the fullness of his swing. On the first hole, waiting to tee off, DiMaggio sat back watching a foursome of college boys ahead swinging with such freedom. 'Oh,' he said with a sigh, 'to have *their* backs.'

DiMaggio and O'Doul were accompanied around the golf course by Ernie Nevers, the former football star, and two brothers who are in the hotel and movie-distribution business. They moved quickly up and down the green hills in electric golf carts, and DiMaggio's game was exceptionally good for the first nine holes. But then he seemed distracted, perhaps tired, perhaps even reacting to a conversation of a few minutes before. One of the movie men was praising the film *Boeing, Boeing*, starring Tony Curtis and Jerry Lewis, and the man asked DiMaggio if he had seen it.

'No,' DiMaggio said. Then he added, swiftly, 'I haven't seen a film in eight years.'

DiMaggio hooked a few shots, was in the woods. He took a No. 9 iron and tried to chip out. But O'Doul interrupted DiMaggio's concentration to remind him to keep the face of the club closed. DiMaggio hit the ball. It caromed off the side of his club, went skipping like a rabbit through the high grass down toward a pond. DiMaggio rarely displays any emotion on a golf course, but now, without saying a word, he took his No. 9 iron and flung it into the air. The club landed in a tree and stayed up there.

'Well,' O'Doul said, casually, 'there goes *that* set of clubs.'

DiMaggio walked to the tree. Fortunately the club had slipped to the lower branch and DiMaggio could stretch up on the cart and get it back.

'Every time I get advice,' DiMaggio muttered to himself, shaking his head slowly and walking toward the pond, 'I shank it.'

Later, showered and dressed, DiMaggio and the others drove to a banquet about ten miles from the golf course. Somebody had said it was going to be an elegant dinner, but when they arrived they could see it was more like a country fair; farmers were gathered outside a big, barnlike building, a candidate for sheriff was distributing leaflets at the front door, and a chorus of homely ladies were inside singing 'You Are My Sunshine'.

'How did we get sucked into this?' DiMaggio asked, talking out of the side of his mouth, as they approached the building.

'O'Doul,' one of the men said. 'It's his fault. Damned O'Doul can't turn *anything* down.'

'Go to hell,' O'Doul said.

Soon DiMaggio and O'Doul and Ernie Nevers were surrounded by the crowd, and the woman who had been leading the chorus came rushing over and said, 'Oh, Mr DiMaggio, it certainly is a pleasure having you.'

'It's a pleasure being here, ma'am,' he said, forcing a smile.

'It's too bad you didn't arrive a moment sooner, you'd have heard our singing.'

'Oh, I heard it,' he said, 'and I enjoyed it very much.'

'Good, good,' she said. 'And how are your brothers Dom and Vic?'

'Fine. Dom lives near Boston. Vince is in Pittsburgh.'

'Why, *hello* there, Joe,' interrupted a man with wine on his breath, patting DiMaggio on the back, feeling his arm. 'Who's gonna take it this year, Joe?'

'Well, I have no idea,' DiMaggio said.

'What about the Giants?'

'Your guess is as good as mine.'

'Well, you can't count the Dodgers out,' the man said.

'You sure can't,' DiMaggio said.

'Not with all that pitching.'

'Pitching is certainly important,' DiMaggio said.

Everywhere he goes the questions seem the same, as if he has some special vision into the future of new heroes, and everywhere he goes, too, older men grab his hand and feel his arm and predict that he could still go out there and hit one, and the smile on DiMaggio's face is genuine. He tries hard to remain as he was – he diets, he takes steam baths, he is careful; and flabby men in the locker rooms of golf clubs sometimes steal peeks at him when he steps out of the shower, observing the tight muscles across his chest, the flat stomach, the long sinewy legs. He has a young man's body, very pale and little hair; his face is dark and lined, however, parched by the sun of several seasons. Still he is always an impressive figure at banquets such as this – an *immortal*, sportswriters called him, and that is how they have written about him and others like him, rarely suggesting that such heroes might ever be prone to the ills of mortal men, carousing, drinking, scheming; to suggest this would destroy the myth, would disillusion small boys, would infuriate rich men who own ball clubs and to whom baseball is a business dedicated to profit and in pursuit of which they trade mediocre players' flesh as casually as boys trade players' pictures on bubblegum cards. And so the baseball hero must always act the part, must preserve the myth, and none does it better than DiMaggio, none is more patient when drunken old men grab an arm and ask, 'Who's gonna take it this year, Joe?'

Two hours later, dinner and the speeches over, DiMaggio is slumped in O'Doul's car headed back to San Francisco. He edged himself up, however, when O'Doul pulled into a gas station in which a pretty redhaired girl sat on a stool, legs crossed, filing her fingernails. She was about twenty-two, wore a tight black skirt and tighter white blouse.

'Look at *that*,' DiMaggio said.

'Yeah,' O'Doul said.

O'Doul turned away when a young man approached, opened the gas tank, began wiping the windshield. The young man wore a greasy white uniform on the front of which was printed the name 'Burt'. DiMaggio kept looking at the girl, but she was not distracted from her fingernails. Then he looked at Burt, who did not recognize him. When the tank was full, O'Doul paid and drove off. Burt returned to his girl; DiMaggio slumped down in the front seat and did not open his eyes again until they'd arrived in San Francisco.

'Let's go see Reno,' DiMaggio said.

'No, I gotta go see my old lady,' O'Doul said. So he dropped DiMaggio off in front of the bar, and a moment later Reno's voice was announcing in the smoky room, 'Hey, here's the Clipper!' The men waved and offered to buy him a drink. DiMaggio ordered a vodka and sat for an hour at the bar talking to a half dozen men around him. Then a blonde girl who had been with friends at the other end of the bar came over, and somebody introduced her to DiMaggio. He bought her a drink, offered her a cigarette. Then he struck a match and held it. His hand was unsteady.

'Is that me that's shaking?' he asked.

'It must be,' said the blonde. 'I'm calm.'

Two nights later, having collected his clothes out of Reno's back room, DiMaggio boarded a jet; he slept crossways on three seats, then came down the steps as the sun began to rise in Miami. He claimed his luggage and golf clubs, put them into the trunk of a waiting automobile, and less than an hour later he was being driven into Fort Lauderdale, past palm-lined streets, toward the Yankee Clipper Hotel.

'All my life it seems I've been on the road travelling,' he said, squinting through the windshield into the sun. 'I never get a sense of being in any one place.'

Arriving at the Yankee Clipper Hotel, DiMaggio checked into the largest suite. People rushed through the lobby to shake hands with him, to ask for his autograph, to say, 'Joe, you look great.' And early the next morning, and for the next thirty mornings, DiMaggio arrived punctually at the baseball park and wore his uniform with the famous No. 5, and the tourists seated in the sunny grandstands clapped when he first appeared on the field each time, and then they watched with nostalgia as he picked up a bat and played 'pepper' with the younger Yankees, some of whom were not even born when, twenty-five years ago this summer, he hit in fifty-six straight games and became the most celebrated man in America.

But the younger spectators in the Fort Lauderdale park, and the sportswriters, too, were more interested in Mantle and Maris, and nearly every day there were news dispatches reporting how Mantle and Maris felt, what they did, what they said, even though they said and did very little except walk around the field frowning when photographers asked for another picture and when sportswriters asked how they felt.

After seven days of this, the big day arrived – Mantle and Maris would swing a bat – and a dozen sports writers were gathered around the big batting cage that was situated beyond the left-field fence; it was completely enclosed in wire, meaning that no baseball could travel more than thirty or forty feet before being trapped in rope; still Mantle and Maris would be swinging, and this, in spring, makes news.

Mantle stepped in first. He wore black gloves to help prevent blisters. He hit right-handed against the pitching of a coach named Vern Benson, and soon Mantle was swinging hard, smashing line drives against the nets, going *ahhh ahhh* as he followed through with his mouth open.

Then Mantle, not wanting to overdo it on his first day, dropped his bat in the dirt and walked out of the batting cage. Roger Maris stepped in. He picked up Mantle's bat.

'This damn thing must be thirty-eight ounces,' Maris said. He threw the bat down into the dirt, left the cage and walked toward the dugout on the other side of the field to get a lighter bat.

DiMaggio stood among the sportswriters behind the cage, then turned when Vern Benson, inside the cage, yelled, 'Joe, wanna hit some?'

'No chance,' DiMaggio said.

'Com'on, Joe,' Benson said.

The reporters waited silently. Then DiMaggio walked slowly into the cage and picked up Mantle's bat. He took his position at the plate but obviously it was not the classic DiMaggio stance; he was holding the bat about two inches from the knob, his feet were not so far apart, and, when DiMaggio took a cut at Benson's first pitch, fouling it, there was none of that ferocious follow through, the blurred bat did not come whipping all the way around, the No. 5 was not stretched full across his broad back.

DiMaggio fouled Benson's second pitch, then he connected solidly with the third, the fourth, the fifth. He was just meeting the ball easily, however, not smashing it, and Benson called out, 'I didn't know you were a choke hitter, Joe.'

'I am now,' DiMaggio said, getting ready for another pitch.

He hit three more squarely enough, and then he swung again and there was a hollow sound.

'Ohhh,' DiMaggio yelled, dropping his bat, his fingers stung, 'I was waiting for that one.' He left the batting cage rubbing his hands together. The reporters watched him. Nobody said anything. Then DiMaggio said to one of them, not in anger nor in sadness, but merely as a simply stated fact, 'There was a time when you couldn't get me out of there.'

1966

Great Men Die Twice

MARK KRAM

There is the feel of a cold offshore mist to the hospital room, a life-is-a-bitch feel, made sharp by the hostile ganglia of medical technology, plasma bags dripping, vile tubing snaking in and out of the body, blinking monitors levelling illusion, muffling existence down to a sort of digital bingo. The Champ, Muhammad Ali, lies there now, propped up slightly, a skim of sweat on his lips and forehead, eyes closed, an almost imperceptible tremor to his arms and head. For all his claims to the contrary, his surface romance with immortality, Ali had a spooky bead on his future; he never saw it sweeping grandly toward him but bellying quietly along the jungle floor. 'We just flies in a room,' he liked to say, moving quickly across the ruins of daily life, plane crashes, train wrecks, matricide, infanticide; then after swatting half of humanity, he'd lower his voice and whisper, as if imparting a secret, 'We just flies, that's all. Got nowhere to fly, do we?'

Images and echoes fill the room, diffuse and speeding, shot through with ineluctable light and the mythopoeic for so long, the glass darkened to a degree no one thought possible; his immense talent, his ring wisdom, his antipathy for chemicals, argued against destructibility; all he would ever do is grow old. For twenty years, while he turned the porno shop of sports into international theatre, attention was paid in a way it never was before or has been since. The crowds were a wonder to behold. Kids scaled the wings of jets to get a glimpse of him; thousands, young and old, tailed him in masses during his roadwork. World leaders marvelled at the spell he cast over the crowds. 'If you were a Filipino,' joked Ferdinand Marcos, 'I'd have to shoot you.' The pope asked for his autograph; Sure, he said, pointing to a picture, but why ain't Jesus black? A young Libyan student in London sat on his bed, kept him up half the night with dithyrambic visions of Muslim revolution. 'Watch, one day you will see,' said Muammar Qaddafi. Half asleep, Ali said: 'Sheeeet, you crazy.' Leonid Brezhnev once dispatched a note to an official at *Izvestia*: 'I would like to see more on Muhammad Ali. Who is this man?'

The Ali Watch: how absurd that it would one day drop down here on a little hospital on Hilton Head Island, South Carolina. The nurse dabs his face dry. What is he thinking? Never has his favourite phrase sounded so dismally precise: *My, my, ain't the world strange.* If he could root back through the maze of moment and incident, would he find premonitory signs sticking out like dire figurations of chicken entrails? Does he remember King Levinsky, one of the many heavy bags for Joe Louis, in the corridor after the Miami Beach weigh-in? Boldly coloured ties draped Levinsky's neck (he sold them on the street), his synapses now like two eggs over-light, in permanent sizzle, as he tried to move into stride with a young Cassius Clay. Over and over, like a one-man Greek chorus, Levinsky croaked, eyes spinning, spittle bubbling from his lips: '*He's gonna take you, kid. Liston's gonna take you, make you a guy sellin' ties . . . Partners with me kid, ya kin be partners with me.*' Does he remember a shadowed evening in his hotel room a day or so after the third Joe Frazier fight, moving to the window, his body still on fire from the assault? He stood there watching the bloodred sun drop into Manila

29

Bay, then took a visitor's hand and guided it over his forehead, each bump sending a vague dread through the fingers. 'Why I do this?' he said softly. Does he remember the Bahamian cowbell tinkling the end of his final, pathetic fight, a derisive good-bye sound stark with omen? What is he thinking?

Ali poses a question, his eyes closed, his lips parting as if he were sliding open manhole covers. 'You die here . . . they take you home?' he asks. The nurses roll their eyes and smile, struck by his innocence; it has nothing to do, they know, with morbidity. He is not joking either. The practical aftermath of death seems to stimulate his curiosity these days; nothing urgent, mind you, just something that begins to get in your mind when you're watching blood move in and out of your body for half the day. Though he is very much a mystic, there is a part of Ali that has always found security and a skewed understanding of life in the quantifiable: amounts, calibrated outcomes, the creaking, reassuring machinery of living. The night before in the hotel lounge, with his wife, Lonnie, beside him, bemusedly aghast, he grilled a pleasant waitress until he knew how many tips she got each week, how many children she had, the frequency of men hitting on her, and the general contour of her reality. 'She have a sad life,' he said later. The nurse now cracks with a deadpan expression: 'You die, we take you home, Muhammad.'

Still, a certain chiaroscuro grimness attaches to their surreal exchange and cries out for some brainless, comic intervention. He himself had long been a specialist in such relief when he would instantly brighten faces during his favourite tours of prisons, orphanages and nursing homes. When down himself (very seldom), he could count on a pratfall from his hysterical shaman, Drew 'Bundini' Brown, on the latest bizarre news from his scheming court, maybe a straight line from some reporter that he would turn into a ricocheting soliloquy on, say, the disgusting aesthetics of dining on pig. No laughs today, though.

'Don't make him laugh,' a nurse insisted when leading a writer and a photographer into the room. 'Laughing shakes the tubing loose.' The photographer is Howard Bingham, Ali's closest friend; he's been with the Champ from the start, in the face of much abuse from the Black Muslims. Ali calls him 'the enemy' or 'the nonbeliever'. His natural instinct is to make Ali laugh; today he has to settle for biting his lower lip and gazing warily back and forth between Ali and his nurses. He doesn't know what to do with his hands. Ali had requested that he leave his cameras outside; just one shot of this scene, of Ali on his back, the forbidding purge in progress, of fame and mystique splayed raw, would bring Bingham a minor fortune. 'He doesn't want the world to see him like this,' says Howard. 'I wouldn't take the picture for a million dollars.'

The process is called plasmapheresis. It lasts five hours and is being conducted by Dr Rajko Medenica. The procedure, popular in Europe, is a cleansing of the blood. Ali is hooked up to an electrocardiograph and a blood–pressure monitor; there is always some risk when blood is not making its customary passage. But the procedure is not dangerous and he is in no pain, we are told. Two things, though, that he surely can't abide about the treatment: the injection of those big needles and the ceaseless tedium. When he was a young fighter, a doctor had to chase him around a desk to give him a shot, and chaotic mobility to him is at least as important as breathing. Bingham can't take his eyes off Ali; the still life of his friend, tethered so completely, seems as incomprehensible to him as it would to others who followed the radiated glow of Ali's invulnerability. The nurses cast an eye at his blood pressure and look at each other. His pressure once jumped twelve points while he watched a TV report on Mike Tyson's street fight with Mitch Green in Harlem. It's rising a bit now,

31

and the nurses think he has to urinate. He can't bear relieving himself in the presence of women; he resists, and his anxiety climbs.

'Ali,' one of them calls. His eyes remain closed, his breathing is hardly audible. The nurse calls to him again; no response. 'Come on now, Ali,' she complains, knowing that he likes to feign death. 'Now, stop it, Ali.' He doesn't move, then suddenly his head gives a small jerk forward and his eyes buck wide open, the way they used to when he'd make some incoherent claim to lineage to the gods. The nurses flinch, or are they in on the joke, too? Eyes still wide, with a growing smile, he says to the writer, weakly: 'You thought I dead, tell the truth. You the only one ever here to see this and I die for ya. You git some scoop, big news round the whole world, won't it be?' He leans his head back on the pillow, saying: 'Got no funny people round me anymore. Have to make myself laugh.' The nurse wants to know if he has to urinate. 'No,' he says with a trace of irritation. 'Yes, you do,' the nurse says. 'Your pressure . . .' Ali looks over at Lonnie with mischievous eyes. 'I just thinkin' 'bout a pretty woman.' The nurse asks him what he'd like for lunch. 'Give him some pork,' cracks Bingham. Ali censures the heretic with a playful stare. Ali requests chicken and some cherry pie with 'two scoops of ice cream'. He turns to the writer again: 'Abraham Lincoln went on a three-day drunk, and you know what he say when he wake up?' He waits for a beat, then says: '"I freed whooooooo?"' His body starts to shake with laughter. The nurse yells: 'Stop it, Muhammad! You'll drive the needles through your veins.' He calms down, rasps, 'I'll never grow up, will I? I'll be fifty in three years. Old age just make you ugly, that's all.'

Not all, exactly; getting old is the last display for the bread-and-circuses culture. Legends must suffer for all the gifts and luck and privilege given to them. Great men, it's been noted, die twice – once as great and once as men. With grace, preferably, which adds an uplifting, stirring, Homeric touch. If the fall is too messy, the national psyche will rush toward it, then recoil; there is no suspense, no example in the mundane. The captivating, aspiring sociopath Sonny Liston had a primitive hold on the equation of greatness. 'Clay [he never called him Ali] beeeg now,' Sonny once said while gnawing on some ribs. 'He flyin' high now. Like an eagle. So high. Where he gonna land, how he gonna land? He gonna have any wings? I wanna see.' Sonny, of course, never made it for the final show. Soon after, he checked out in Vegas, the suspicion of murder hovering over the coroner's report.

Who wanted to ask the question back then, or even be allowed to examine in depth its many possibilities? It was too serious for the carnival, immediately at odds with the cartoon bombast that swirled around Ali, the unassailable appeal of the phenomenon, the breathtaking climb of the arc. Before him, the ring, if not moribund, had been a dark, sombre corner of sports, best described by the passing sight of then-middleweight-king Dick Tiger, leaving his beat-up hotel wearing a roomy black homburg and a long pawnshop overcoat, a black satchel in his hand, heading for the subway and a title fight at the Garden. But the heavyweight champions – as they always will – illuminated the image sent out to the public. There was the stoic, mute Joe Louis, with his cruising menace; the street fighter Rocky Marciano, with his trade-unionist obedience; the arresting and dogged Floyd Patterson, who would bare his soul to a telephone pole at the sight of a pencil; all unfrivolous men who left no doubt as to the nature of their work.

With the emergence of Muhammad Ali, no one would ever see the ring the same way again, not even the fighters themselves; a TV go, a purse, and a sheared lip would never be enough; and a title was just a belt unless you did something with it. A fighter had to *be*; a product, an event, transcendental. Ali and the new age met stern, early resistance. He was the demon loose at a holy rite. With his preening narcissism, braggart mouth and stylistic quirks, he was viewed as a vandal of ring tenets and etiquette. Besides, they said, he couldn't punch, did not like to get hit, and seemed to lack a sufficient amount of killer adrenalin. True, on the latter two counts. 'I git no pleasure from hurtin' another human bein',' he used to say. 'I do what I gotta do, nothin' more, nothin' less.' As far as eating punches, he said, 'Only a fool wanna be hit. Boxin' just today, my face is forever.' Others saw much more. The ballet master Balanchine, for one, showed up at a workout and gazed in wonder. 'My God,' he said, 'he fights with his legs, he actually fights with his legs. What an astonishing creature.' Ali's jab (more like a straight left of jolting electricity) came in triplets, each a thousandth of a second in execution. He'd double up cruelly with a left hook (rarely seen) and razor in a right – and then he'd be gone. Even so, it took many years for Ali to ascend to a preeminent light in the national consciousness. In the Sixties, as a converted Black Muslim, he vilified white people as blond, blue-eyed devils. His position on Vietnam – 'I ain't got no quarrel with those Vietcong, anyway. They never called me nigger' – was innocent at first, but then taken up as if he were the provocateur of a national crisis. The politicians, promoters, and sweeping sentiment converged to conspire against his constitutional right to work: states barred him from fighting. He resisted the draft and drifted into exile. Three years later he returned, heavier, slower, but with a new kind of fire in his belly. Though he had defeated heavyweight champion Sonny Liston and defended his title nine times, Ali had never had a dramatic constituency before. Now a huge one awaited him, liberals looking for expression, eager literati to put it in scripture, worn-out hippies, anyone who wanted to see right done for once. The rest is history: the two symphonic conflicts with Joe Frazier; the tingling walk with him into the darkness of George Foreman. Then, the Hegelian 'bad infinite' of repeating diminishing cycles: retiring, unretiring, the torture of losing weight, the oiling of mushy reflexes. The margins of dominance compressed perilously, and the head shots (negligible before exile) mounted.

Greatness trickled from the corpus of his image, his career now like a gutshot that was going to take its time before killing. His signing to fight Larry Holmes, after retiring a second time, provoked worried comment. After watching some of Ali's films, a London neurologist said that he was convinced Ali had brain damage. Diagnosis by long distance, the promoters scoffed. Yet among those in his camp, the few who cared, there was an edginess. They approached Holmes, saying, 'Don't hurt him, Larry.' Moved, Holmes replied: 'No way. I love Ali.' With compassion, he then took Ali apart with the studied carefulness of a diamond cutter; still, not enough to mask the winces at ringside. Ali failed to go the route for the first time in his career. Incredibly, fourteen months later, in 1981, his ego goaded him to the Bahamas and another fight, the fat jellied on his middle, his hand-speed sighing and wheezing like a busted old fan; tropic rot on the trade winds. Trevor Berbick, an earnest plug, outpointed him easily. Afterward, Angelo Dundee, who had trained Ali from the start and had to be talked into showing up for this one, watched him slumped in the dressing room, then turned away and rubbed his eyes as certain people tried to convince Ali that he had been robbed and that a fourth title was still possible.

The public prefers, indeed seems to insist on, the precedent set by Rocky Marciano, who quit undefeated, kept self-delusion at bay. Ali knew the importance of a clean farewell, not only as a health measure but as good commercial sense. His ring classicism had always argued so persuasively against excessive physical harm, his pride was beyond anything but a regal exit. But his prolonged decline had been nasty, unseemly. Who or what pressured him to continue on? Some blamed his manager, Herbert Muhammad, who had made millions with Ali. Herbert said that his influence wasn't that strong.

Two years after that last fight, Ali seemed as mystified as everyone else as to why he hadn't ended his career earlier. He was living with his third wife, the ice goddess Veronica, in an L.A. mansion, surrounded by the gifts of a lifetime – a six-foot hand-carved tiger given to him by Teng Hsiao-ping, a robe given to him by Elvis Presley. Fatigued, his hands tremoring badly, he sat in front of the fire and could only say: 'Everybody git lost in life. I just git lost, that's all.'

Now, five years later, the question *why* still lingers, along with the warning of the old aphorism that 'we live beyond what we enact'. The resuscitation of Ali's image has been a sporadic exercise for a long time now, some of it coming from friends who have experienced heartfelt pain over his illness. Others seem to be trying to assuage a guilt known only to themselves, and a few are out to keep Ali a player, a lure to those who might want to use his name in business; though the marketplace turns away from billboards in decline. Not long ago, a piece in *The New York Times Magazine* pronounced him the Ali of old, just about terminally perky. Then, Ali surfaced in a front-page telephone interview in the *Washington Post*. He appeared to have a hard grasp on politics, current states' rights issues and federal judgeships being contested – a scenario that had seemed as likely as the fusillade of laser fire Ali said Muslim spaceships would one day loose on the white devils.

Noses began to twitch. What and who was behind the new Ali, the wily Washington lobbyist who had the ear of everyone from Strom Thurmond to Orrin Hatch? The wife of Senator Arlen Specter even baked Ali a double-chocolate-mousse pie. For a good while, most of these senators, and others, knew only the voice of Ali on the phone. Dave Kindred, a columnist for the *Atlanta Journal-Constitution* who has known Ali since his Louisville days, concluded that it was most likely Ali's attorney, Richard Hirschfeld, widely regarded as a brilliant impersonator of Ali, who had made the calls. (Hirschfeld has refused to comment on whether or not he did so.) Hirschfeld and Ali had cut up a lot of money over the years on numerous enterprises (funded by other people), from hotels to cars, most of them failing. Ali's lobbying seemed to centre on a federal judgeship for a Hirschfeld friend, and a federal lawsuit in which Ali sought $50 million in damages from his 'wrongful conviction in the 1967 draft evasion case'. He lost the suit but succeeded in getting Senator Hatch and others to explore a loophole that might remedy the verdict. Ali eventually had to materialize (with Hirschfeld hard by his side), and many on Capitol Hill were unable to match the man with the voice. One of Sam Nunn's aides, noting Ali's listlessness and Hirschfeld's aggressive quizzing, wondered: 'Is Ali being carted around like a puppet?' Certainly a serpentine tale; but had Ali been a collaborator all along?

At his farm in Berrien Springs, Michigan, Ali sits at the end of a table in the living room. The 247 pounds of weight have made him a bit short of breath. He's battled his appetite (two, three desserts, meals back to back) and sedentary lapses for years. Several months before, he had been almost sleek, thanks to fourteen-mile walks and his wife's efforts to police him at the table. But what is disturbing is the general profile of his condition.

For a long time now, he has appeared indifferent to the ravages of his problem. But he dispels that notion when asked how seriously he considered a dangerous brain operation in Mexico before his family talked him out of it. 'Scale of ten,' he says, 'a six.' The answer reflects the terrible frustration that must exist within him, the daily, fierce struggle with a body and mind that will not capitulate to his bidding. He sits there, his hands shaking, his movements robotic, the look on his face similar to what the Marines call a thousand-yard stare.

Why is it, do you think, that after all these years, the dominant sound around Ali is silence? Look at the cataract of noise caught by TV sound men, look at the verbosity that snared some novelists into thinking he was a primitive intelligence capable of Ciceronian insight. Part of the fever of the times; if the Black Panther Huey Newton, posing with rifle and spear, could be written up as a theoretical genius and his partner, Bobby Seale, interpreted as a tactical wizard, then how much a symbol was Ali, the first to tap and manifest glinting black pride, to dispute with vigour erosive self-laceration.

The fact was that he was not cerebral; he was a reflex of confusing emotions and instant passions. He did have street cunning, most of it aimed at keeping himself a mystery. 'People like mystery,' he used to say. 'Who is he? What's he all about? Who's he gonna be tomorrow?' To that end, he tossed the media rabble dripping hunks of redundant, rote monologue; his loudness provided a great show and diverted probing questions. By nature, he was a gentle, sensitive man, and even in the throes of angry threats against whites it was hard to hide a smile, for he loved what the blacks call 'selling wolf tickets', tricking people into fear. The Black Panthers used that gambit well, and the TV crews followed their presence. Thinking of all this, how could someone so alien to ideas and thought, who communicated privately, in scraps and remote silences, be capable of fooling Washington politicians? Absurd, of course, but then the question emerges: Did he allow himself to be used?

'How about all those phone calls?' he is asked.

'What calls?' he responds, vacantly.

'To politicians this past summer.'

'You can't believe that,' he says. 'Man wrote that, he's a cracker from way back in Louisville. Always hated blacks.'

'But the piece had the goods.'

'I'm signin' my autographs now,' he says. 'This the only important thing in my life. Keepin' in touch with the people.'

'Were you used?'

'Spend a hundred dollars on stamps every week. Give 'em all my autograph that write me.'

'Were you used?'

'For what?'

'To influence your lawsuit.'

'I ain't worried about money,' he says.

'Maybe you just want to be big again. Remember what you told Elvis. "Elvis, you have to keep singin' or die to stay big. I'm gonna be big forever."'

He smiles thinly: 'I say anything shock the world.'

'You like politics now?'

'Politics put me to sleep.'

'You were at the Republican National Convention.'

'You borin' me, putting me to sleep.'

'Reagan, Hatch, Quayle, they would've clapped you in jail in the old days.'

His eyes widen slightly: 'That right?' He adds: 'I'm tired. You better than a sleepin' pill.'

But don't let the exchange mislead. Ali is not up to repartee these days, never was, really, unless he was in the mood, and then he'd fade you with one of his standard lines ('You not as dumb as you look'). He speaks very, very slowly, and you have to lean in to hear him. It takes nearly an hour to negotiate the course of a conversation. Typically, he hadn't been enlightening on the Capitol Hill scam. Over the years, he has been easily led, told by any number of rogues what his best interests were. If the advisers were friends who appealed to his instinct to help them move up a rung, he was even more of a setup. Later, Bingham says: 'Ali was pissed about that impersonation stuff. He had no idea.' Why didn't he just say that he didn't make the calls? 'You know him,' he says. 'He'll never betray who he thinks has tried to help him. The idea that people will think less of him now bothers him a lot.'

If there was ever any doubt about the staying power of Ali, it is swept aside when you travel with him. His favourite place in the world – next to his worktable at his farm – is an airport. So he should be in high spirits now; he'll be in three airports before the day's over. But he's a bit petulant with Lonnie, who aims to see that he keeps his date at Hilton Head Island. He can't stand hospitals. They get in the way of life. He found it hard even to visit his old sidekick Bundini when he was dying. Paralysed from the neck down, Bundini could only move his eyes. Ali bent down close to his ear and whispered: 'You in pain?' The eyes signalled 'yes'. Ali turned his head away, then came back to those eyes, saying: 'We had some good times, didn't we?' Bundini's eyes went up and down. Ali talks about this in the Chicago airport. He's calmed down now, sits off by himself, ramrod-straight and waiting. He wears a pinstripe suit, red tie, and next to him is his black magician's bag; he never lets it out of his sight. The bag is filled with religious tracts already autographed; which is the first thing he does every day at 6.00 a.m., when he gets up. All he has to do is fill in the person's name.

His autograph ritual and travel are his consuming interests. He'll go anywhere at the ring of a phone, and he spends much time on the road. Perhaps the travel buoys him; he certainly gets an energy charge from people. Soon they begin to drop like birds to his side. 'You see,' he says, 'all I gotta do is sit here. Somethin', ain't it? Why they like me?' He is not trying to be humble, he is genuinely perplexed by the chemistry that exists between himself and other people. 'Maybe they just like celebrities,' he says. Maybe, he's told, he's much more than a celebrity. He ponders that for a moment, and says: 'That right?' By now, a hundred people have lined up in front of him, and a security guard begins to keep them in line. Ali asks them their name, writes, then gives them his autographed tracts. Some ask him to pose for pictures, others kid him about unretiring. He raises his fist: 'Kong [Mike Tyson], I'm comin' after you.' Near the end, he does a magic trick for a lady, using a fake thumb. 'Where you going, Muhammad?' she asks. He thinks, and then leans over to the writer and asks: 'Where we going?' The lady's eyes fill, she hugs him and says: 'We love you so much.' What is it that so movingly draws so many people – his innocent, childlike way, the stony visual he projects, set off against his highly visible symptoms?

That night over dinner, Ali's eyes open and close between courses. He fades in and out of the conversation, has a hint of trouble lifting the fork to his mouth. His every day includes periods like this, he's in and out like a faraway signal. Sometimes he's full of play. He likes to swing his long arm near a person's ear, then create a friction with thumb and forefinger to produce a cricket effect in the ear. Then the play is gone, and so is he. 'One day,' Lonnie is saying, 'I want someone to catch his soul, to show what a fine human being he is.' Ali says, head down: 'Nobody know me. I fool 'em all.' Lonnie is Ali's fourth wife. She was a little girl who lived across from Ali's old Louisville home when he was at the top. She is a woman of wit and intelligence, with a master's degree in business administration. She plans his trips, is the tough cop with him and his medicine, and generally seems to brighten his life. Ice cream dribbles down Ali's chin. 'Now, Muhammad,' she says, wiping it away. 'You're a big baby.' He orders another dessert, then says: 'Where are we?' A blade of silence cuts across the table.

Bingham says: 'Hilton Head Island.'

Ali says: 'Ya ever wake up and don't know where you are?' Sure, he is told, steady travel can make a person feel like that for an instant; yet it is obvious that short-term memory for him is like a labyrinth.

Ali's day at the hospital is nearly over. He will soon be counting down the minutes. Right now he's in high spirits. A nurse has secretly slipped him some strips of paper. He has a complete piece of paper in his hands. He crumples the paper, pretends to put it in his mouth, then billows his cheeks until he regurgitates tiny pieces all over his chest. 'Ain't magic a happy thing,' he says, trying to contain his giggling. When Dr Medenica comes, Ali jokes with him. The doctor goes about examining the day's results. He looks at the bags of plasma: 15,000 ccs have been moved through Ali. Floyd Patterson has expressed dismay over the current treatment. 'No brain damage?' Floyd had said. 'Next you'll be hearing he was bit by a cockroach. He's gonna kill Clay . . . He'll drop dead in a year.' Medenica bridles at the comment. 'He's rather ignorant. I'm going to have to call that man.' Ali wants to know what Patterson said. Nobody wants to tell him. 'Tell me,' says Ali. Everyone looks at each other, and someone finally says: 'Floyd says you'll drop dead in a year.' Ali shrugs it off: 'Floyd mean well.'

It is Medenica's contention that Ali suffers from pesticide poisoning. Though his work has met with some scepticism in the medical community, Medenica is respected in South

Carolina. His desk is rimmed with pictures of prominent people
– a senator, a Saudi prince, an ambassador – patients for whom
he has retarded death by cancer. He is supposed to have done
wonders for Marshal Tito of Yugoslavia. Tito was so grateful,
he arranged funding for Medenica's clinic in Switzerland.
When he died, the funds were cut off and Medenica was left
with bills and criminal indictment by the Yugoslavians and the
Swiss. 'Don't ask how Ali got the pesticides,' Medenica says.

Plasmapheresis is a solid treatment for pesticide poisoning,
which occurs more than ever these days. The blood cleaning
removes the immune complex, which in turn removes toxins.
But how can Medenica be so sure that Ali's problem is not
brain damage? Dr Dennis Cope, of UCLA, has said that Ali
is a victim of 'Parkinson's syndrome secondary to pugilistic
brain syndrome'. In short, he took too many head shots.
Medenica, though, is a confident man.

He predicts Ali will be completely recovered. 'I find absolutely no brain damage. The magnetic resonator tests show
no damage. Before I took him as a patient, I watched many
of his fight films. He did not take many head blows.'

Is he kidding?

'No, I do not see many head blows. When he came this
summer, he was in bad shape. Poor gait. Difficult speech.
Vocal-cord syndrome, extended and inflamed. He is much
better. His problem is he misses taking his medicine, and he
travels too much. He should be here once a month.'

Finally, Ali is helped out of his medical harness. He dresses
slowly. Then, ready to go out, he puts that famous upper-
teeth clamp on his bottom lip to show determination and
circles the doctor with a cocked right fist. His next stop is for
an interferon shot. It is used to stimulate the white blood
cells. Afterward, he is weak, and there is a certain sadness in
his eyes. On the way to the car, he is asked if the treatment
helps. He says: 'Sheeeet, nothin' help.'

The Lincoln Town Car moves through the night. Bingham, who is driving, fumbles with the tape player. Earlier in the day he had searched anxiously for a tape of Whitney Houston doing 'The Greatest Love of All', a song written especially for Ali years ago. He had sensed that Ali would be quite low when the day was over, and he wanted something to pick him up. The words, beautiful and haunting, fill the car.

> *Everybody's searching for a hero,*
> *People need someone*
> *To look up to,*
> *I never found anyone who*
> *Fulfilled that need;*
> *A lonely place to be,*
> *So I learned to depend on me.*
> *I decided long ago*
> *Never to walk in anyone's shadow;*
> *If I fail, if I succeed,*
> *At least I lived as I believe,*
> *And no matter what*
> *They take from me,*
> *They can't take away my dignity;*
> *Because the greatest love of all*
> *Is happening to me.*
> *I found the greatest love of all*
> *Inside of me.*
> *The greatest love of all is easy*
> *To achieve,*
> *Learning to love yourself is*
> *The greatest love of all.**

'You hear that,' Bingham says, his voice cracking. 'Everything's gonna be just fine, Ali.'

The dark trees spin by. There is no answer. What is he thinking?   1989

44

Michael Jordan Leaps the Great Divide

JOHN EDGAR WIDEMAN

'This old woman told me she went to visit this old retired bullfighter who raised bulls for the ring. She had told him about this record that had been made by a black American musician, and he didn't believe that a foreigner, an American – and especially a black American – could make such a record. He sat there and listened to it. After it was finished, he rose from his chair and put on his bullfighting equipment and outfit, went out and fought one of his bulls for the first time since he had retired, and killed the bull. When she asked him why he had done it, he said he had been so moved by the music that he just had to fight the bull.' – Miles: *The Autobiography*

When it's played the way it's spozed to be played, basketball happens in the air, the pure air; flying, floating, elevated above the floor, levitating the way oppressed peoples of this earth imagine themselves in their dreams, as I do in my lifelong fantasies of escape and power, finally, at last, once and for all, free. For glimpses of this ideal future game we should thank, among others, Elgin Baylor, Connie Hawkins, David Thompson, Helicopter Knowings, and of course, Julius

Erving, Dr J. Some venerate Larry Bird for reminding us
how close a man can come to a perfect gravity-free game and
still keep his head, his feet firmly planted on terra firma. Or
love Magic Johnson for confounding boundaries, conjuring
new space, passing lanes, fast-break and break-down lanes
neither above the court nor exactly on it, but somehow
whittling and expanding simultaneously the territory in which
the game is enacted. But really, as we envision soaring and
swooping, extending, refining the combat zone of basketball
into a fourth, outer, other dimension, the dreamy ozone
of flight without wings, of going up and not coming down
till we're good and ready, then it's Michael Jordan we
must recognize as the truest prophet of what might be
possible.

A great artist transforms our world, removes scales from our
eyes, plugs from our ears, gloves from our fingertips, teaches
us to perceive reality differently. Proust said of his countryman
and contemporary, the late-nineteenth-century Impressionist
Auguste Renoir: 'Before Renoir painted there were no
Renoir women in Paris, now you see them everywhere.' Tex
Winters, a veteran Chicago Bulls coach, a traditionalist who
came up preaching the conventional wisdom that a lay-up is
the highest-percentage shot, enjoys Michael Jordan's dunks,
but, says MJ, 'Every time I make one, he says, "So whatever
happened to the simple lay-up?" "I don't know, Tex, this is
how I've been playing my whole career." You know, this
stuff here and this stuff here [the hands are rocking, cradling,
stuffing an imaginary ball] is like a lay-up to me. You know
I've been doing that and that's the creativity of the game
now. But it drives him nuts . . . and he says, "Well, why
don't you draw the foul?" I say I never have. The defence
alters many of my shots, so I create. I've always been able to
create in those situations, and I guess that's the Afro-American

game I have, that's just natural to me. And even though it may not be the traditional game that Americans have been taught, it works for me. Why not?'

The lady is gaudy as Carnival. Magenta, sky-blue, lime, scarlet, orange swirl in the dress that balloons between her sashed waist and bare knees. Somebody's grandmother, gift-wrapped and wobbly on Madison Street, toreadoring through four lanes of traffic converging on Chicago Stadium. Out for a party. Taxi driver says this is where they stand at night. Whore women, he calls them, a disgusted judgmental swipe in his voice, which until now has been a mellow tour-guide patter, pointing out the Sears Tower, Ditka's, asking me how tall is Michael Jordan. The tallest in basketball? Laughing at his memory of a photo of Manute Bol beside Muggsy Bogues. Claiming to have seen Michael Jordan at Shelter, a West Side club late on Wednesday, the night of Game Four after the Bulls beat Detroit last spring to even the best-of-seven NBA championship semifinal at two games apiece. Yes, with two other fellas. Tall like him. Lots of people asking him to sign his name. Autographs, you know. A slightly chopped, guttural, Middle-Eastern-flavoured Chicagoese, patched together in the two and a half years he's resided in the States. 'I came here as student. My family sent me three thousand dinars a year, and I could have apartment, pay my bills, drive a car. Then hard times at home. Dinar worth much less in dollars. Four people, all of them, must work a month to earn one thousand dinars. No school now. I must work now. American wife and new baby, man.'

The driver's from Jordan, but the joke doesn't strike me until I'm mumbling out the cab in front of Chicago Stadium. JORDAN, the country. Appearing in the same column, just above JORDAN, MICHAEL, in *Readers' Guide to Periodical Literature*, where I researched Michael Jordan's career. Usually more entries in each volume under JORDAN, MICHAEL, than any other JORDAN.

The other passenger sharing a cab from O'Hare to down-town Chicago is a young German from Hamburg, in the city with about one hundred thousand fellow conventioneers for the Consumer Electronics Show. It's while he's calculating exchange rates to answer the driver's question about the cost of a Mercedes in Germany that the lady stumbles backward from the kerb into the street, blocking strings of cars pulled up at a light. She pirouettes. Curtsies. The puffy dress of many colours glows brighter, wilder against greys and browns of ravaged cityscape. Partially demolished or burnt-out or abandoned warehouses and storefronts line both sides of Madison. Interspersed between buildings are jerry-rigged parking lots where you'd leave your car overnight only if you had a serious grudge against it. I think of a mouth rotten with decay, gaps where teeth have fallen out. Competing for the rush of ballgame traffic, squads of shills and barkers hip-hop into the stalled traffic, shucking and jiving with anyone who'll pay attention. One looms at the window of our cab, sandwiched in, a hand-lettered sign tapping the windshield, begging us to park in his oasis, until the woman impeding our progress decides to attempt the kerb again and mounts it this time, Minnie Mouse high heels firmly planted as she gives the honk-ing cars a flounce of Technicolor behind and a high-fived middle finger.

The woman's black, and so are most of the faces on Madison as we cruise toward the stadium in a tide of cars carrying white faces. Closer, still plenty of black faces mix into the crowd – vendors, scalpers, guys in sneakers and silky sweat suits doing whatever they're out there doing, but when the cab stops and deposits me into a thin crust of dark people who aren't going in, I cut through quickly to join the mob of whites who are.

I forget I am supposed to stop at the press trailer for my credentials but slip inside the building without showing a pass or a ticket because mass confusion reigns at the gate. Then I discover why people are buzzing and shoving, why the gate crew is overwhelmed and defeated: Jesse Jackson. Even if it belongs to Michael Jordan this evening, Chicago's still Jackson's town too. And everyone wants to touch or be touched by this man who is instantly recognized, not only here in Chicago but all over the world. Casually dressed tonight, black slacks, matching black short-sleeved shirt that displays his powerful shoulders and arms. He could be a ballplayer. A running back, a tight end. But the eyes, the bearing are a quarterback's. Head high, he scans the whole field, checks out many things at once, smiles, and presses the flesh of the one he's greeting but stays alert to the bigger picture. When a hassled ticket-taker stares suspiciously at me, I nod toward Jesse, as if to say, I'm with him, he's the reason I'm here, and that's enough to chase the red-faced gatekeeper's scrutiny to easier prey. This minute exchange, insignificant as it may be, raises my spirits. Not because Jesse Jackson's presence enabled me to get away with anything – after all, I'm legit, certified, qualified to enter the arena – but because the respect, the recognizability he's earned reflects on me, empowers me, subtly alters others' perceptions of who I am, what I can do. When I hug the Reverend Jesse Jackson I try to impart a little of my appreciation to the broad shoulders I grip. By just being out there, being heard and seen, by standing for something – for instance, an African-American man's right, duty and ability to aim for the stars – he's saved us all a lot of grief, bought us, black men, white, the entire rainbow of sexes and colours, more time to get our sorry act together. *Thank you* is what I always feel the need to say when I encounter the deep light of his smile.

Your town, man.

Brother Wideman, what are you doing here?

Writing about Michael Jordan.

We don't get any further. Somebody else needs a piece of him, a word, a touch from our Blarney stone, our Somebody.

In Michael's house the PA system is cranked to a sirenlike, earsplitting pitch, many decibels higher than a humane health code should permit. The Luvabulls, Chicago's aerobicized version of the Dallas Cowboy Cheerleaders, shake that fine, sculpted booty to pump up the fans. Very basic here. Primal-scream time. The incredible uproar enters your pores, your blood, your brain. Your nervous system becomes an extension of the overwhelming assault upon it. In simplest terms, you're ready for total war, transformed into a weapon poised to be unleashed upon the enemy.

From my third-row-end-zone folding chair, depth perception is nil. The game is played on a flat, two-dimensional screen. Under the opposite basket the players appear as they would crowded into the wrong end of a telescope.

Then, as the ball moves toward the near goal, action explodes, a zoom lens hurtles bodies at you larger, more intense than life. Middle ground doesn't exist. You're surprised when a ref holds up both arms to indicate a three-point goal scored from beyond the twenty-three-foot line. But your inability to gauge the distance of jump shots or measure the swift, subtle penetration, step by step, yard by yard, as guards dribble between their legs, behind the back, spinning, dipping, shouldering, teasing their way upcourt, is compensated for by your power to watch the glacial increments achieved by big men muscling each other for position under your basket, the intimacy of those instants when the ball is in the air at your end of the court and just about everybody on both teams seems driven to converge into a space not larger than two telephone booths. Then it's grapple, grunt and groan only forty feet away. You can read the effort, the fear, the focus in a player's eyes. For a few seconds you're on the court, sweating, absorbing the impact, the crash of big bodies into one another, wood buckling underfoot, someone's elbow in your ribs, shouts in your ear, the wheezes, sighs, curses, hearing a language spoken here and nowhere else except when people are fighting or making love.

MJ: What do I like about basketball? *Hmmm*. That's a good question. I started when I was twelve. And I enjoyed it to the point that I started to do things other people couldn't do. And that intrigued me more. Now I still enjoy it because of the excitement I get from fans, from the people, and still having the same ability to do things that other people can't do but want to do and they can do only through you. They watch you do it, then they think that they can do it. Or maybe they know it's something they can't do and ironically, that's why they feel good watching me. That drives me. I'm able to do something that no one else can do.

And I love competition. I've earned respect thanks to basketball. And I'm not here just to hand it to the next person. Day in and day out I see people take on that challenge, to take what I have earned. Joe Dumars, for one – I mean, I respect him, don't get me wrong. It's his job. I've got something that people want. The ability to gain respect for my basketball skills. And I don't ever want to give it away. Whenever the time comes when I'm not able to do that, then I'll just back away from the game.

JW: We've always been given credit for our athletic skill, our bodies. You've been blessed with exceptional physical gifts, and all your mastery of the game gets lost in the rush. But I believe your mind, the way you conceive the game, plays as large a role as your physical abilities. As much as any other player I've seen, you seem to play the game with your mind.

MJ: The mental aspect of the game came when I got into college. After winning the national championship at North Carolina in 1982, I knew I had the ability to play on that level, but there were a lot of players who had that ability. What distinguishes certain players from others is the mental aspect. You've got to approach the game strong, in a mental sense. So from my sophomore year on, I took it as a challenge to try and out-think the defence, outthink the next player. He might have similar skills, but if I can be very strong mentally and really determined mentally, I can rise above most opponents. As you know, I went through college ball with Coach Dean Smith, and he's a very good psychological-type coach. He doesn't yell at you. He says one line and you think within yourself and know that you've done something wrong . . . When I face a challenger, I've got to watch him, watch what he loves to do, watch things that I've done that haven't worked . . . How can I come up with some weapon, some other surprises to overpower them?

JW: You don't just use someone on your team to work two-on-two. Your plan seems to involve all ten players on the court. A chesslike plan for all four quarters.

MJ: I think I have a good habit of evaluating situations on the floor, offensively, defensively, teammate or opponent. And somehow filling in the right puzzle pieces to click. To get myself in a certain mode or mood to open a game or get a roll going. For instance, the last game we lost to Detroit in the playoffs last spring: we're down twenty, eighteen, twenty-two points at the half. Came back to eleven or ten down. I became a point guard. Somehow I sensed it, sensed no one else wanted to do it or no one else was going to do it until I did it. You could see once I started pushing, started doing these things, everybody else seemed like they got a little bit higher, the game started to go higher, and that pushes my game a little higher, higher, higher. I kept pulling them up, trying to get them to a level where we could win.

Then, you know, I got tired, I had to sit out and rest. Let Detroit come all the way back. It hurts a little bit, but then again I feel good about the fact that I mean so much to those guys, in a sense that if I don't play, if I don't do certain things, then they're not going to play well. It's like when people say it's a one-man gang in Chicago. I take it as a compliment, but then it's unfair that I would have to do all that.

I can dictate what I want to do in the course of the game. I can say to my friends, Well, I'll score twelve points in the first quarter . . . then I can relax in the second quarter and score maybe six, eight. Not take as many shots, but in the second half I can go fifteen, sixteen, quick. That's how much confidence I have in my ability to dictate how many points I can score and be effective and give the team an opportunity to win.

I don't mind taking a beating or scoring just a few points in the first half, because I feel the second half I'm going to have the mental advantage. My man is going to relax. He feels he's got an advantage, he's got me controlled, that means he's going to let down his guard just a little bit. If I can get past that guard one time I feel that I've got the confidence to break him down.

On the same night in July that Michael Jordan slipped on a damp outdoor court at his basketball camp on the Elmhurst College campus, jamming his wrist and elbow, on a court in a park called Mill River in North Amherst, Massachusetts, my elbow cracked against something hard that was moving fast, so when I talked with Michael Jordan the next morning in Elmhurst, Illinois, on the outskirts of Chicago, my elbow was sore and puffy, his wrapped and packed in ice.

We'd won two straight in our pickup, playground run,

pretty ordinary, local, tacky hoop that's fine if you're inside the game, but nothing to merit a spectator's attention. Ten on the court, nine or ten on the sidelines hanging out or waiting to take on the winners, a small band of witnesses, then, for something extraordinary that happened next. On a breakaway dribble Sekou beats everybody to the hoop except two opponents who hadn't bothered to run back to their offensive end. It was that kind of game, spurts of hustle, lunch breaks while somebody else did the work. Sekou solo, racing for the hoop, two defenders converging to cut him off, slapping at the ball, bodying him into a vise to stop his momentum. What happens next is almost too quick to follow. Sekou picks up his dribble about eight feet from the basket, turns his back to the goal, to the two guys who are clamping him, as if, outnumbered, he's looking downcourt for help. A quick feint, shoulders and head dipped one way, and then he brings the ball across his body, slamming it hard against the asphalt, *blam*, in the space his fake has cleared. Ball bounds higher than the basket and for an instant I think he's trying a trick shot, bouncing the ball into the basket, a jive shot that's missing badly as the ball zooms way over the rim toward the far side of the backboard. While I'm thinking this and thinking Sekou's getting outrageous, throwing up a silly, wasteful, selfish shot even for the playground, even in a game he can dominate because he's by far the best athlete, while I'm thinking this and feeling a little pissed off at his hotdogging and ball hogging, the ball's still in the air, and Sekou spins and rises, a pivot off his back foot so he's facing the hoop, one short step gathering himself, one long stride carrying him around the frozen defenders and then another step in the air, rising till he catches the rock in flight and crams it one-handed down, *down* through the iron.

Hoop, poles and backboard shudder. A moment of stunned silence, then the joint erupts. Nobody can believe what they've seen. The two players guarding Sekou kind of slink off. But it wasn't about turning people into chumps or making anybody feel bad. It was Sekou's glory. Glory reflected instantly on all of us because he was one of us out there in the game and he'd suddenly lifted the game to a higher plane. We were all larger and better. Hell, none of us could rise like Sekou, but he carried us up there with him. He needed us now to amen and goddamn and high-five and time-out. Time out, stop this shit right here. Nate, the griot, style-point judge, and resident master of ceremonies, begins to perform his job of putting into words what everybody's thinking. *Time out.* We all wander on to the court, to the basket that's still vibrating, including the two guys Sekou had rocked. Sekou is hugged, patted, praised. Skin smacks skin, slaps skin. Did you see that? Did you see that? I ain't never seen nothing like that. Damn, Sekou. Where'd you learn that shit? Learned it sitting right here. Right here when I was coming up. My boy Patrick. Puerto Rican dude, you know Patrick. He used to do it. Hey man, Patrick could play but Patrick didn't have no serious rise like that, man. Right. He'd bounce it, go get it, shoot it off the board. Seen him do it more than once. Sitting right here on this bench I seen him do it. Yeah, well, cool, I can believe it. But man that shit you did. One hand and shit . . . damn . . . damn, Sekou.

I almost told Michael Jordan about Sekou's move. Asked Michael if he'd ever attempted it, seen it done. Maybe, I thought, someday when I'm watching the Bulls on the tube Michael will do a Sekou for a national audience and I won't exactly take credit, but deep inside I'll be saying, Uh-huh, uh-huh. Because we all need it, the sense of connection, the feeling we can be better than we are, even if better only through someone else, an agent, a representative, Mother Teresa, Mandela, one of us ourselves taken to a higher power, altered for a moment, alive in another's body and mind. One reason we need games, sports, the heroes they produce. To rise. To fly.

I didn't have to tell Michael Jordan Sekou's story. MJ earns a living by performing nearly on a regular basis similar magical feats for an audience of millions across the globe. I told him instead about my elbow. Tuesday night had been a bad night for elbows all over North America. Commiserating, solicitous about his injury, but also hopelessly vain, proud of mine, as if our sore elbows matched us, blood brothers meeting at last, a whole lifetime of news, gossip and stuff to catch up on. Since we couldn't very well engage in that one-on-one game I'd been fantasizing, not with him handicapped by a fat elbow, we might as well get on with the interview I'd been seeking since the end of the NBA playoffs. Relax and get it on in this borrowed office at Elmhurst, my tape recorder on the desk between us, Michael Jordan settled back in a borrowed swivel chair, alert, accommodating. Mellow, remarkably fresh after a protracted autograph session, signing one item apiece for each of the 350 or so campers who'd been sitting transfixed in a circle around him earlier that morning as he shared some of his glory with them in a luminous exchange that masked itself as a simple lesson in basketball basics from Michael Jordan.

JW: Your style of play comes from the playground, comes from tradition, the African-American way of playing basketball.

MJ: Can't teach it.

JW: When I was coming up, if a coach yelled 'playground move' at you it meant there was something wrong with it, which also meant in a funny way there was something wrong with the playground, and since the playground was a black world, there was something wrong with you, a black player out there doing something your way rather than their way.

MJ: I've been doing it my way. When you come out of high school, you have natural, raw ability. No one coaches it, I mean, maybe nowadays, but when I was coming out of high school, it was all natural ability. The jumping, quickness. When I went to North Carolina, it was a different phase of my life. Knowledge of basketball from Naismith on ... rebounds, defence, free-throw shooting, techniques. Then, when I got to the pros, what people saw was the raw talent I'd worked on myself for eleven, twelve years *and* the knowledge I'd learned at the University of North Carolina. Unity of both. That's what makes up Michael Jordan's all-around basketball skills.

JW: It seems to me we have to keep asserting the factors that make us unique. We can't let coaches or myths about body types take credit for achievements that are a synthesis of our intelligence, physical gifts, our tradition of playing the game a special way.

MJ: We were born to play like we do.

JW: Players like you and Magic have transformed the game. Made it more of a player's game, returned it closer to its African-American roots on the playground.

MJ: You know, when you think about it, passing like Magic's is as natural, as freewheeling, as creative as you can be. You can call it playground if you want, but the guy is great. And certainly he's transcended the old idea of point guard. You never saw a six-eight, six-nine point guard before he came around. No coach would ever put a six-eight guy back there.

JW: If you were big, you were told to go rebound, especially if you were big and black.

MJ: Rebound. Go do a jump lay-up, be a centre, a forward. A man six-eight started playing, dribbling in his backyard. Said, I can do these things. Now look. Everybody's trying to get a six-nine point guard.

JW: For me, the real creativity of the game begins with the playground. Like last night, watching young guys play, playing with them, that's where the new stuff is coming from. Then the basketball establishment names it and claims it.

MJ: They claim it. But they can't. The game today is going away from the big guy, the old idea everybody's got to have a Jabbar, Chamberlain. Game today is going toward a versatile game. Players who rebound, steal, block, run the court, score, the versatile player who can play more than one position. Which Magic started. Or maybe he didn't start it, but he made it famous. This is where the game's going now.

JW: Other people name it and claim it. That kind of appropriation's been a problem for African-American culture from the beginning. Music's an obvious example. What kind of music do you like?

MJ: I love jazz. I love mellow music. I love David Sanborn. Love Grover Washington Jr. Rap . . . it's okay for some people. But huh-uh. Not in my house.

JW: Do you listen to Miles Davis?

MJ: Yeah.

JW: He talks about his art in a new biography he wrote with Quincy Troupe. When Miles relates jazz to boxing, I also hear him talking about writing, my art, and basketball, yours.

MJ: I know what you're saying.

JW: Right. There's a core of improvisation, spontaneity in all African-American arts.

MJ: I'm always working to put surprises, something new in my game. Improvisation, spontaneity, all that stuff.

What's in a name: *Michael* — archangel, conqueror of Satan. 'Now war arose in heaven. Michael and his angels fighting against the dragon; and the dragon and his angels fought, but they were defeated' (Revelation 12:7); *Jordan* – the foremost river in Palestine, runs from the Lebanons to the Dead Sea, 125 miles, though its meanderings double that length. 'Jordan water's bitter and cold . . . chills the body, don't hurt the soul . . .' (African-American traditional spiritual). *Michael Jordan* – a name worth many millions per annum. What's in that name that makes it so incredibly valuable to the people who have millions to spend for advertising what they sell, who compete for the privilege of owning, possessing Michael Jordan's name to adorn or endorse their products? In a country where Willie Horton's name and image helped win (or lose) a presidential election, a country in which one out of every four young black males is in prison, on parole or probation, a country where serious academics convene to consider whether the black male is an endangered species, how can we account for Michael Jordan's enormous popularity? Because MJ is an American of African descent, isn't he? Maybe we're more mixed up about race than we already know we are. Perhaps MJ is proof there are no rules about race, no limits to what a black man can accomplish in our society. Or maybe he's the exception that proves the rule, the absence of rules. The bedrock chaos and confusion that dogs us. At some level we must desire the ambiguity of our racial thinking. It must work for us, serve us. When one group wants something bad enough from the other, we reserve the right to ignore or insist upon the inherent similarities among all races, whichever side of the coin suits our purposes. One moment colour-blind, the next proclaiming one group's whiteness, the other's blackness, to justify whatever mischief we're up to. It's this flip-flopping that defines and perpetuates our race problem. Our national schizophrenia and disgrace. It's also the door that allows MJ entry to superstardom, to become a national hero, our new DiMaggio, permits him to earn his small fraction of the billions we spend to escape rather than confront the liabilities of our society.

Sports Illustrated offers a free Michael Jordan video if you subscribe right away. Call today. In this ad, which saturates prime time on the national sports network, a gallery of young people, male and female, express their wonder, admiration, awe and identification with Michael Jordan's supernatural basketball prowess. He can truly fly. The chorus is all white, good-looking, clean cut, casually but hiply dressed. An audience of consumers the ad both targets and embodies. A very calculated kind of wish fulfilment at work. A premeditated attempt to bond MJ with these middle-class white kids with highly disposable incomes.

In other ads, black kids wear fancy sneakers, play ball, compete to be a future Michael Jordan. There's a good chance lots of TV viewers who are white will enter the work force and become dutiful, conspicuous consumers, maybe even buy themselves some vicarious flight time by owning stuff MJ endorses. But what future is in store for those who intend to *be* the next MJ? Buy Jordan or be Jordan. Very different messages. Different futures, white and black. Who's zooming who?

In another national ad, why do we need the mediating figure of an old, distinguished-looking, white-haired, Caucasian gentleman in charge, giving instructions, leading MJ into a roomful of kids clamouring for MJ's magic power?

The Palace at Auburn Hills, the Detroit Pistons' home, contrasts starkly with Chicago Stadium. Chicago, the oldest NBA arena; the Palace one of the newest. Chicago Stadium is gritty, the Palace plush. In the Auburn Hills crowd an even greater absence of dark faces than in Chicago Stadium. But they share some of the same fight songs. *We will, we will, rock you.* And the Isley Brothers' classic 'Shout'. On a massive screen in the centre of the Palace, cuts from the old John Belushi flick *Animal House* drive the Detroit fans wild. 'Shout' is background music for an archetypal late-Fifties, early-Sixties frat party. White college kids in togas twist and shout and knock themselves out. Pre-Vietnam American Empire PG-rated version of a Roman orgy. A riot of sloppy boozing, making out, sophomoric antics to the beat of a jackleg, black rhythm-and-blues band that features a frenzied, conk-haired singer, sweating, eyes rolling, gate-mouthed, screaming, 'Hey-ay, hey-ay. Hey-ay, hey-ay, shout! C'mon now, shout.' Minstrel auctioneer steering the action higher, higher. Musicians on the screen performing for their audience of hopped-up, pampered students fuse with the present excitement, black gladiators on the hardwood floor of the Palace revving up their whooping fans. Nothing is an accident. Or is it? Do race relations progress, or are we doomed to a series of reruns?

JW: What's the biggest misconception that is part of your public image? What's out there, supposedly a mirror, but doesn't reflect your features?

MJ: I'm fortunate that there are no big misunderstandings. My biggest concern is that people view me as being some kind of a god, but I'm not. I make mistakes, have faults. I'm moody, I've got many negative things about me. Everybody has negative things about them. But from the image that's been projected of me, I can't do any wrong. Which is scary. And it's probably one of the biggest fears I have. And I don't know how to open people's eyes. I mean, I'm not going to go out and make a mistake so that people can see I make mistakes. Hey, you know, I try to live a positive life, love to live a positive life, but I do have negative things about me and I do make mistakes. And I'm so worried that if I make a mistake today, it can ruin the positive things I try to project. It's a day-in, day-out, nine-to-five job.

JW: A lot of pressure.

MJ: Pressure I didn't ask for, but it was given to me and I've been living, living with it.

JW: A kind of trap, isn't it, because you say, 'I don't want everybody to think I'm a paragon of virtue. I'm a real person.' But you also know in the back of your mind being a paragon is worth X number of dollars a day. So you don't like it but you profit from it.

MJ: Right. It has its advantages as well as disadvantages. Advantages financially. I'm asked to endorse corporations that are very prestigious as well as very wealthy. I have the respect of many, many kids as well as parents, their admiration. So it's not *just* the financial part. You said the financial part, but the respect that I earn from the 350 kids in this camp and their parents, friends, equals the financial part of it. The respect I get from those people – that's the pressure.

JW: Not to let them down.

MJ: Not to let them down.

Post-game Chicago Stadium. Oldest arena in the league. Old-fashioned bandbox. Exterior built on monumental, muscle-flexing scale. Inside you have to duck your head to negotiate a landing that leads to steep steps descending to locker rooms. Red painted walls, rough, unfinished. Overhead a confusion of pipes, wires – the arteries of the beast exposed. Ranks of folding chairs set up for post-game interviews. MJ breaks a two-day silence with the media. Annoyed that the press misinterpreted some animated exchanges between teammates and himself.

None of the usual question-and-answer interplay. MJ says his piece and splits, flanked by yellow-nylon-jacketed security men, three of them, polite but firm, benign sheep dogs guarding him, discouraging the wolves.

In MJ's cubicle near the door hangs a greenish suit, a bright tropical-print shirt, yellows, black, beige, oranges, et cetera. He's played magnificently, admonished the press, clearly weary, but the effort of the game's still in his eyes, distracting, distancing him, part of him still in another gear; maybe remembering, maybe savouring, maybe just unable to cut it loose, the flow, the purity, the high of the game when every moment counts, registers, so as he undresses, the yellow jacket assigned to his corner has to remind him not to get naked, other people are in the room.

A man chatting up the security person screening MJ's cubicle holds a basketball for MJ to sign. As MJ undresses he's invited to a reporter's wedding. The soon-to-be groom is jiving with another member of the press, saying something about maybe having a kid will help him settle down, improve his sense of responsibility. MJ, proud father of two-year-old Jeffrey Michael, interrupts. 'You got to earn the respect of kids. Responsibility and respect, huh-uh. You don't just get it when you have a kid. Or a couple kids.'

Word's sent in that Whitney Houston and her entourage are waiting next door for a photo session. Celebrity hugging and mugging. I say hi to a man hovering near MJ's corner. Thought he might be MJ's cut buddy or an older brother. Turns out to be MJ's father. Same dark, tight skin. Same compact, defined physique. 'Yes, I think I'm Mister Jordan. Hold on a minute, let me check my social security card.' A kidder like his son. Like his son, he gives you friendly pats. Or maybe it's son like father. In the father's face, a quality of youthfulness and age combined, not chronological age but the timeless serenity of a tribal elder, a man with position, authority, an earned place in a community. In the locker room of the Spectrum in Philly, I'd been struck by the same mix in MJ's face as he addressed reporters. Unperturbed by lights, cameras, mikes, the patent buzz and jostle of media rudeness swarming around him, he sits poised on a shelf in a dressing stall, his posture unmistakably that immemorial high-kneed, flex-thighed, legs-widespread, weight-on-the-buttocks squat of rural Africans. Long hands dangling between his knees, head erect, occasionally bowing as he retreats into a private, inner realm to consider a question, an answer before he spoke. Dignified, respectful. A disposition of body learned how many grandfathers ago, in what faraway place. Passed on, surviving in this strange land.

From the shower MJ calls for slip-ons. Emerges wrapped in a towel. A man, an African-American man in a suit of dark skin, tall, broad-shouldered, long-limbed, narrow-waisted, bony ankles and wrists, his body lean-muscled, sleek, race cars, cheetahs, a computer-designed body for someone intended to sprint and leap, loose and tautly strung simultaneously, but also, like your body and mine, a cage. MJ is trapped within boundaries he cannot cross, you cannot cross. No candid camera needs to strip him any further. Why should it? Whose interests would be served? Some of his business is not ours. Are there skeletons in his closet? Letters buried in a trunk, sealed correspondence? What are we seeking with our demands for outtakes, for what's X-rated in public figures' lives? In the crush of the locker room, one reporter (a female) whispers to another; we build these guys up so we can be around to sell the story when they fall.

Naked MJ. A price on his head. He pays it. We pay it. Hundreds of thousands of fans plunk down the price of a ticket to catch his act live. Millions of dollars are spent to connect products with the way this body performs on a basketball court. What about feedback? If body sells products, how do products affect body? Do they commodify it, place a price on it? Flesh and blood linked symbiotically with products whose value is their ability to create profit. If profit's what it's all about — body, game, product — does profit-making displace ballplaying? Are there inevitable moments when what's required of MJ the ballplayer is different from what's required of the PR Jordan created by corporate interests for media consumption?

The PR Michael Jordan doesn't need to win a ring. He's already everything he needs to be without a ring. Greatest pressure on him from this perspective is to maintain, replicate, duplicate whatever it is that works, sells. It's an unfunny joke when MJ says wryly, 'Fans come to see me score fifty and the home team win.' The PR Jordan doesn't really lose when he has a spectacular game and his teammates are mediocre. He's still MJ. But if he puts forth a kamikaze, all-or-nothing, individual effort and fails by forcing or missing shots, by coming up short, the blame falls squarely on his shoulders. If he plays that tune too often, will the public continue to buy it?

Can a player be bigger than the game? Is Jordan that good? Does he risk making a mockery of the game? (Recall John Lennon. His lament that the Beatles' early, extraordinary success pressured them to repeat themselves, blunted artistic innovation, eventually pushed them into self-parody, the songs they'd written taking over, consuming them.)

The young man from Mississippi, baby of eleven children, speaks with a slow, muddy, down-home drawl. We're both relaxing in the unseasonably warm sun, outside Hartford, the Bradley International Airport B Terminal. My destination: Chicago, Game Six of last spring's NBA Eastern Championship. He's headed for his sister's home in Indiana. A nice place, he hopes. Time to settle down after five, six years of roaming, but decent work's hard to find. 'I sure hope Michael wins him a ring. Boy, I want to see that. Cause my man

Michael's the best. Been the best awhile. He's getting up there a little bit in age, you know. Ain't old yet but you know, he can't do like he used to. Used to be he could go out anytime and bust sixty-three. He's still good, still the best now but he better go on and get him his ring.'

JW: I'm jumping way back on you now. Laney High School, Wilmington, N.C., the late Seventies, early Eighties. How did it feel to sit on the bench?

MJ: I hated it . . . you can't help anybody sitting on the bench. I mean, it's great to cheer, but I'm not that type of person. I'm not a cheerleader.

JW: You couldn't make the team?

MJ: I was pissed. Because my best friend, he was about six-six, he made the team. He wasn't good but he was six-six and that's tall in high school. He made the team and I felt I was better . . . They went into the playoffs and I was sitting at the end of the bench and I couldn't cheer them on because I felt I should have been on the team. This is the only time that I didn't actually cheer for them. I wanted them to lose. Ironically, I wanted them to lose to prove to them that I could help them. This is what I was thinking at the time: You made a mistake by not putting me on the team and you're going to see it because you're going to lose. Which isn't the way you want to raise your kids . . . but many kids now do think that way, only because of their desire to get out and show that they can help or they can give something.

I think to be successful, I think you have to be selfish, or else you never achieve. And once you get to your highest level, then you have to be unselfish. When I first came to the league, I was a very selfish person in the sense I thought for myself first, the team second . . . and I still think that way in a sense. But at the same time, individual accolades piled up for me and were very soothing to the selfishness that I'd had in myself. They taught me how, you know, to finally forget about the self and help out the team, which is where I am now. I always wanted the team to be successful but I felt, selfishly, I wanted to be the main cause.

> Phi Gamma Delta was assailed Monday with charges of racism, becoming the second fraternity to face such accusations stemming from activities during Round-Up last weekend.
>
> At the root of the newest charges is a T-shirt sold and distributed by the fraternity – often known as the Fijis – during its annual 'low-hoop' basketball tournament Saturday. On the T-shirt is the face of a 'Sambo' caricature atop the body of professional basketball player Michael Jordan.
>
> Meanwhile, Delta Tau Delta continued its internal investigation into Friday's incident in which FUCK COONS and FUCK YOU NIGS DIE were spray-painted on a car destroyed with sledgehammers on fraternity property . . .
>
> – *The Daily Texan*, University of Texas, Austin, 4/10/90

We're slightly lost. My wife and I in a rental car on the edge of Shreveport, Louisiana, leading two rented vans carrying the Central Massachusetts Cougars. We're looking for the Centenary College Gold Dome, where soon, quite soon, opening ceremonies of the AAU Junior Olympic Girls Basketball national tourney will commence. Suddenly we cross Jordan Street, and I know we'll find the Gold Dome, be on time for the festivities, that my daughter, Jamila, and her Cougar teammates will do just fine, whatever. Renoir women everywhere, Jordans everywhere.

Next day, while girls of every size, shape, colour, creed and ethnic background, from nearly every state in the Union, are playing hoop in local high school gyms, about three miles from the Cougars' motel, at the Bossier City Civic Center, Klansmen in hoods and robes distribute leaflets at a rally for former Klan leader David Duke, who's running for the US Senate.

MJ: Well, I think real often in terms of role models, in terms of positive leaders in this world . . . Nelson Mandela, Bill Cosby . . . We're trying to show there are outlets, there are guidelines, there are positive things you can look for and achieve. I mean, we're trying to give them an example to go for. I think that's the reason I try to maintain the position I have in the corporate world as well as in the community. That we can do this, prove that success is not limited to certain people, it's not limited to a certain colour . . . Grab a hand and pull someone up. Be a guide or a role model. Give some type of guidelines for other people to follow.

JW: What ways do you have of controlling this tidal wave of public attention? How do you remain separate from the Michael Jordan created 'out there'?

MJ: Stay reachable. Stay in touch. Don't isolate. I don't try to isolate myself from anybody. I think if people can feel that they can touch or come up and talk to you, you're going to have a relationship and have some influence on them. My old friends, who I try to stay in touch with at all times, I think they always keep me close to earth.

About six years ago I was only forty-three, so I couldn't understand why the jumper was falling short every time, banging harmlessly off the front of the iron. After a summer-camp game my wife, Judy, had watched mainly because our sons, Dan and Jake, were also playing, I asked her if she'd noticed anything unusual about my jump shot. 'Well, not exactly,' she offered, 'except when you jumped your feet never left the ground.'

JW: When you're playing, what part of the audience is most important to you?

MJ: Kids. I can notice a kid enjoying himself. On the free-throw line, *bing*, that quick, I'll wink at him, smile, lick a tongue at him, and keep going and still maintain the concentration that I need for the game. That's my personality. I've always done it. I can catch eye-to-eye a mother, a father, anybody . . . kid around with them as I'm playing in a serious and very intense game. That's the way I relax, that's the way I get my enjoyment from playing the game of basketball. Seeing people enjoying themselves and relating to them like I'm enjoying myself. Certainly letting them know they're part of the game.

The game. I am being introduced to a group of young African-American men, fifteen or so high school city kids from Springfield, Massachusetts, who are attending the first-ever sessions of a summer camp at Hampshire College, an experiment intended to improve both their basketball skills and SAT scores. My host, Dennis Jackson (a coach, coincidentally, at Five-Star hoop camp back when Michael Jordan, still a high schooler, made his debut into the national spotlight), is generously extolling my credentials – author, professor, college ballplayer, Rhodes scholar – but it isn't till Dennis Jackson says this man is working on an article about MJ that I know I have everybody's attention. I tell them that I haven't received an interview with MJ yet, he's cooling out after the long season, but they're eager to hear any detail of any MJ moment I've been privy to so far. An anecdote or two and then I ask them to free-associate. When I say MJ what comes to mind first? *Air, jam, slam-dunk, greatest, wow* are some of the words I catch, but the real action is in faces and bodies. No one can sit still. Suddenly it's Christmas morning and they're little boys humping down the stairs into a living room full of all they've been wishing for. Body English, *ohhs* and *ahhs*. Hey man, he can do anything, anything. DJ assures me that if Mike promised, I'll get my interview. *As good a player as MJ is, he's ten times the person.* We're all in a good mood, and I preach a little. Dreams. The importance of believing in yourself. My luck in having a family that supported me, instilled the notion I was special, that I could do anything, be anything. Dreams, goals. Treasuring, respecting the family that loves you and stands behind you.

What if you don't have no family?

The question stops me in my tracks. Silences me. I study each face pointed toward me, see the guys I grew up with, my sons, brothers, Sekou, MJ, myself, the faces of South African kids *toi-toing* in joy and defiance down a dirt street in Crossroads. I'd believed the young men were listening, and because I'd felt them open up, I'd been giving everything I had, trying to string together many years, many moments, my fear, anger, frustration, the hungers that had driven me, the drumbeat of a basketball on asphalt a rhythm under everything else, patterning the crazy-quilt chaos of images I was trying to make real, to connect with their lives. What if there's no family, no person, no community out there returning, substantiating the fragile dream a young man spins of himself? Silenced.

Michael said he didn't like politics. I'll always stand up for what I think is right, but . . . Politics, he said, was about making choices. And then you get into: This side's right and that side's wrong. Then you got a fight on your hands. Michael's friends say he naturally shies away from controversy. He's mellow. Middle-of-the-road. Even when the guys are just sitting around and start arguing about something,

Michael doesn't like it. He won't take sides, tries to smooth things out. That's Michael.

Finally I respond to the young man at the circle's edge leaning back on his arms. He doesn't possess an NBA body. He may be very smart, but that can be trouble as easily as salvation. You have me, I want to say. I support you, love you, you are part of me, we're in this together. But I know damn well he's asking for more. Needs more. Really, he's asking for nothing while he's asking everything.

Find a friend. I bet you have a cut buddy already. Someone to hang with and depend on. One person who won't let you fall. And you won't let him fall. Lean on each other. It's hard, hard, but just one person can make a difference sometimes.

They look at the books I've written. Ask more questions. Mostly about Michael again. Some eyes are drifting back to the court. This rap's been nice, but it's also only a kind of intermission. The game. I should have brought my sneaks. Should be thirty years younger. But why, seeing the perils besetting these kids, would anyone want to be thirty years younger? And why, if you're Peter Pan playing a game you love and getting paid a fortune for it and adored and you can fly too, why would you ever want to grow a minute older?

The young men from Springfield say hello.

Nate, the historian from the court at Mill River, said: 'Tell the Michael I say hello.'

1990

And Then He Kissed Me

GORDON BURN

This has to begin where the story of real-time English football begins — at Hillsborough, on the day when ninety-five Liverpool supporters were crushed to death in April 1989.

Sean O'Hara was there, supporting Nottingham Forest in an FA Cup semi-final that, for the second year running, had seen Forest drawn against Liverpool.

Sean O'Hara was twenty in 1989 and had already supported Forest for fourteen years. It hadn't been an automatic choice for a six-year-old. Many of his friends growing up in the Bestwood area of Nottingham in those years supported Liverpool or Man U. 'Glory-hunters', Sean called them.

His football-going days started with the arrival of Brian Clough as manager at the City Ground. Clough had laid the foundation of his legend at Derby, slumbering at the bottom of the second division when he took over, and transformed by him into League Champions within three years.

He would put the same kind of heat under Nottingham Forest, a club solidly on course for the third division in 1975. That was part of the pact with the missing thousands who had failed to flock to the City Ground for generations.

They included David (always known as Stan) O'Hara, Sean's father, a building labourer who was converted from a sceptic to a believer when the new appointment was announced. He assured his son that Cloughie was a top man, bound to lead them to glory. As an act of faith, Stan O'Hara went and had FOREST tattooed up each arm.

Cloughie was a manager who delivered; he put hardware on the sideboard. But even if you ignored his on-field achievements, the stuff of his hero appeal was obvious. Here was a character of whimsical impulse and savage ego; a man who went at things free-style.

He'd walked away from Derby County when the chairman had tried to get him to button his lip on non-sporting topics like Biafra, Watergate, Vietnam, the NHS. He was that rare creature in association football, a hairy-chested socialist.

He had distributed free tickets for matches to picketing miners and regularly docked the players' wages at Derby for contributions to Oxfam.

At Nottingham, he'd have one season where an exclusive interview was the price of a wheelchair (and many more where it was the price of a generous consignment of the Lanson that may today account for his permanently high colour and dewlapped champagne chins).

But most compelling of all, perhaps, in a popular hero, Cloughie had a personal tragedy in his back story. Playing for Sunderland against Bury on an iced-over pitch on Boxing Day, 1962, he smashed his right knee in a way that effectively ended his career. He had scored two hundred and fifty-one goals in two hundred and seventy-four matches. He was twenty-six.

It is part of the legend that he cried for three years, until the fourth division's bottom club, Hartlepool United, gave him the job as the youngest League manager. At that point he had been in danger of disappearing into the bottle.

Stan O'Hara's father-in-law, Sean's grandfather, was in the stands on the day Cloughie collided with the Bury goalkeeper.

He saw him go down; watched him being carried off. It gave Sean, who believes he has never had any luck in his life – he'll tell you this – an extra emotional investment in Cloughie's life.

Sean O'Hara was unemployed in 1989, as he had been (as he still is) since leaving school. He was also the father of a ten-month-old son, Shane. Jenny, Sean's mother, who works as an orderly in an old people's home, ran up the street after him as he set off to watch Nottingham Forest against Liverpool at Hillsborough, to give him five of her last seven pounds. 'I was always, like, our mum's favourite,' Sean says. 'I used to get owt off of her.'

Mrs O'Hara heard the first word about the Hillsborough disaster from her next-but-one neighbour, whose husband was also at Sheffield. 'We stood at the gate,' she remembers, 'and – what was it? – I think there was fifteen dead then. I started work at four, and when I arrived it was forty-summat dead. By quarter-past seven, it was more than sixty. I went down the pub that night and sat wi' me mate and she told me they reckoned it was over eighty, and still rising.

'And then that night we seen it on the telly. Ours had come back. But there's so many kids in Liverpool didn't come back. So many tragedies. All right, we don't like the football team, I know. But they're working class like us, and football's a working-class game. It's not lardee-das like show-jumping an' that. So it hit every working-class home, didn't it? It could have been ours just the same as theirs. So much sadness. A lifetime of memories. All for a game of bloody football.'

Sean O'Hara has a sister, Tracy, who is twenty, and a brother, Patrick, eleven. Patrick suffers from asthma and is constantly in and out of hospital. It was because of Patrick's asthma that Sean, his girlfriend Sandra and their baby Shane were eventually given a house of their own by the council.

Tonight, though, Patrick is sprawled on the floor watching the video of *Roger Rabbit*. He's wearing the full Forest strip, plus a pair of surfer baggies over the silver tracksuit trousers. Draped over a wooden clothes-horse in a corner is a second Forest shirt with its Tricky Tree symbol, Shipstone's Fine Beer slogan and diamond-shaped Umbro logo.

'He cries when they lose,' Patrick's mother says, 'just like Sean used to at his age. He'd come home and sit and cry. Since you've been six, Brian Clough has been . . .'

'God.' Sean finishes her sentence.

'I don't like him when he's being mouthy,' Mrs O'Hara continues. 'But, personally thinking, round here Cloughie's every kid's idol. I mean, Sean worshipped him. Pat worships him now. And that's twelve years after.'

The O'Hara household is, as you'd expect, stuffed full of Cloughie-connected keepsakes and memorabilia. But pride of place is reserved for the video that Patrick is reluctantly loading into the machine now (he's seen it played so often he can recite it – intro, voice-over, Q and A, sign-off – from memory).

Nobody believed Sean O'Hara when he told them he'd been fisted by Cloughie. The mates who had been with him at the City Ground for the Littlewoods Cup quarter-final against Queen's Park Rangers that night in January 1989 refused to believe him for the whole of the long walk home.

He hardly believed it himself: that the person who had connected with a useful left hook just as he was about to have it away on his toes after joining in an invasion of the pitch – he'd jumped on Lee Chapman's back, pumped Steve Hodge's hand, stood in the centre circle waving his arms – was the person whose constant (but distant) presence and pronouncements had given a continuity to his life.

But of course there it was – here it is – in living colour, in freeze-frame, in SloMo; the back-swing, the moment of impact, the reaction shot. It happened on a Wednesday night. By Thursday, Sean was learning first-hand what it was like to be part of a celebrity culture.

It was as if the punch had knocked a hole in the screen that separated mediated life – Cloughie's high-visibility, two hundred and forty thousand pound-a-year life – from dole-wallah-lived life. Brian Clough and Sean O'Hara were on tape together and had the same value. Their names sat side by side in the papers.

'I was on the Central news at six o'clock. Headlines. "Youth Hit by Cloughie Speaks to Central." Doo-doo-do-de-do. Like that. Next morning it was "Clough Knocked Stuffing out of Me" on the front page of the *Mirror*. Jeezus.'

Immediately Sean sensed a rift with his friends at the Unemployed Club, who saw him in a new light. They believed he was pocketing Cloughie-sized fees and failing to spread it around. But it was what happened next, the continuing media fall-out, that was truly mind-blowing.

As his brother fast-forwards, shadow images of Sean show up in the pattern of interference and the muck of distortion. The real Sean, meanwhile, busies himself with Shane in the part of the room farthest from the television.

Brian Clough is as well-known for his leeriness of foreigners and homosexuals as he is for being a dressing-room dictator. Forest players are not allowed to kiss on the pitch. They can shake hands after a goal, exchange high fives. But there must be no embracing, no flying-scissor clinches, no physical involvement. Gary McAllister refused to sign for Forest, after Leicester City had accepted the million-pound offer for him, because the manager wanted to know if he was gay, when he said he wasn't married.

So you can imagine the confusion Sean O'Hara felt when he became the object of Cloughie's first screen kiss.

Actually, to be strictly accurate, he was his second. Forty-eight hours after being cuffed by Clough, Sean and another of the pitch invaders, Jim McGowan, were invited by the BBC to the City Ground where, they were told, Brian Clough was going to apologize on-camera for his actions.

The first thing that happened was that they were installed in a small room with a bottle of wine – the 'about a-pound-a-bottle kind' – and Sean was instructed to remove the earrings, a hoop and a stud that he has worn since he was at school. He was told Brian Clough wouldn't see him wearing earrings.

Now Clough's face fills the screen – full and flushed, the eyes small and puffy, as if he has been driving into the sun for several hours. Now he is offering his cheek first to Jim McGowan and then to Sean and saying 'Gizzakiss.'

'Chase me!' McGowan says as he plants a smacker on the manager. But Sean isn't smiling as he steps forward. I look over at him now and he isn't watching.

His family thinks Sean was taken out for a meal by Cloughie after the filming was over. They think that, because that's what Sean has always told them. But earlier, sitting in a pub chatting, before going on to his mother's, he has admitted that this was a story concocted to cover what he still regards as his humiliation.

More than two years on, he still gets asked for autographs by younger Forest supporters. But he also hears 'Gizzakiss!' from cars as he is waiting at bus-stops or walking through town. 'Whooooo! Cloughie's bum boy!'

'I mean, I can't go nowhere, really,' Sean had said. 'Not even now. I come in here tonight an' they were all recognizing me, looking at me like that. You can see 'em look. Everywhere you go.'

Different managers handle pressure differently. Kenny Dalglish imploded, suffering from success fatigue. And Cloughie, the longest-serving manager in British football, has started kicking out the jams by kissing men on television.

Since kissing Sean, he has kissed the television interviewer Gary Newbon and called his team a bunch of pansies. Earlier this year, he kissed the ball-boys at Crystal Palace and has started kissing other managers after the final whistle.

Three months separated Sean's close encounter with Cloughie and the Hillsborough tragedy. He had seen his first dead bodies at Hillsborough; corpses being carried away: hard men weeping.

Before we got up to go, I asked him to consider carefully the following: what had had the most impact on his life – Hillsborough, or being drawn into the orbit of Cloughie? He answered immediately.

'Hillsborough was a bad sight. I saw a few dead bodies. I went into shock like everybody else for a while. But as far as its effect on my life, it doesn't compare to Cloughie. But it's just one of them things, innit? I mean, I didn't ask to be on the telly. One minute you're cast as a down-and-out 'cause you ain't got a job. The next you're The Boy Who Got Kissed By Cloughie.

'They kept saying do this, do that, stand here, move there. And I was thinking: what am I doing down here? I thought of telling him to piss off in that second. But at the time I just kissed him.'

1991

The Shame of Argentina

COLM TOIBIN

The Buenos Aires police came for him when he was still sleeping. Once they had the warrant to search the house, they had begun to ring around journalists and television crews: the address, they said, is Calle Franklin 869, and the raid will be between two and three in the afternoon. You might be interested, they said, because Diego Maradona is inside.

He had been up most of the night playing *chin-chon*, a local version of rummy, with two friends. Friends from the old days, who enjoyed his power and his money. One of them was known as El Soldado – the soldier – because he tended to do whatever Maradona wanted when they were out on the town. At some stage the previous evening, three young women had visited the apartment; two stayed and enjoyed themselves with Maradona and his friends, but the other left early.

She may or may not have been a police informer. She may or may not have phoned the police. But by the following morning the police knew who was in the apartment – and that there was cocaine, which those inside had been consuming that night.

That was Friday, April 26, 1991. On Monday, Argentina's main sports magazine, *El Grafico*, reported the police had found Maradona asleep in bed, naked beside one of his friends. That report caused much righteous indignation in Buenos Aires. But it was untrue. Maradona was alone in bed when the police came, and he was wearing underpants. He was asleep, curled up in a foetal position.

By the time the police entered the apartment, the evidence went, one of Maradona's companions had thrown a nylon packet of cocaine out of the window, and it had landed on the awning over the shop below. It contained two or three grams of cocaine. The police had a witness who said he saw it being thrown from the window of the apartment in which Maradona was sleeping. That such a witness was so easily found and so willing to come forward makes the raid on Calle Franklin 869 seem a set-up to get Maradona, and Buenos Aires buzzes with theories about the reasons for the raid: to distract the public from the scandals surrounding President Carlos Menem's wife's family; to impress the American Embassy, increasingly perturbed by evidence that Argentina, rich in private air-strips, is being used as a centre for cocaine distribution and that Menem's family is involved.

Maradona had been living it up since he slipped out of Italy on April 1, using the diplomatic passport he had been given by President Menem before the 1990 World Cup. Suddenly, for the first time in his life, he was in Buenos Aires without any training schedule or daily routine. For three weeks, he had been free to do as he pleased. When he was arrested, his family had not seen him for two days.

Some of his soccer friends have remained intensely loyal. Sergio Batista, who played with him in the 1986 World Cup and shared a room with him in Italy during the 1990 tournament, turned up in court to support him, and has been seeing him and training with him since then. Batista believes Maradona has never come to realize fully what his name means, what being Maradona entails. He loves it, the fame, the adulation, but he has never fully understood, Batista says, just how limited the rest of his life would have to be.

Batista did not see much of Maradona during the first weeks back in the city, nor did Maradona see many of his close friends from sport. He hung around instead with people more interested in what Argentinians used to call *samba y caramba* than in keeping fit or playing football. There is, in Argentina, a deep disapproval of drug-consumption, as there is a disapproval of alcohol (Maradona hardly touches alcohol). It is eminently possible, perhaps the most likely scenario, that Diego Maradona and his activities came to the attention of the police in Buenos Aires over and over again in the weeks before his arrest. It is entirely possible that there was no government-sponsored conspiracy to get him. It could be that he simply left himself wide open, innocently misunderstanding how far he could go in his home town.

The night of his arrest he was scheduled to attend a huge party to celebrate the National Day of Sport. Carlos Menem, ex-President Raúl Alfonsín and the entire Argentinian sports establishment would be there. He was the hero come home as victim. Up to his arrest, he had had everyone's sympathy.

But now you could watch him on television being led out of the flat by police. People remembered he had been involved in an anti-drugs advertising campaign just eighteen months before. He had suddenly joined the list of people whom Argentinians blame for the terrible despair that overwhelms their country.

'Who is representing whom?' Hans Henningson asked. It was early 1976, in the Sheraton Hotel in Buenos Aires. These two youngsters had come to meet Henningson and Juan Carlos Cazaux to discuss sponsorship from Puma, for which both men worked. The two youngsters were so small and raw. One was dark and open-faced; the other was pudgy with curly fair hair. He was introduced as the *representante*; he walked with a limp.

No Argentinian player had ever had an agent before. It was unheard of. But even then it was clear that the player, the dark, open-faced one, Diego Maradona, was exceptional; even then he stood out. Juan Carlos Cazaux had first heard about him the previous year, but wasn't interested in offering him sponsorship. Maradona was too young at fifteen to be taken on.

And there were other reasons for not going to see him. He had come to fame not as a footballer but as a performer. He was the small boy who came out at half-time with a football and moved around the pitch, to wild cheers and applause, keeping the ball in the air, using his feet and his head with incredible skill, never letting the ball get beyond his control. They loved this kid, he could do amazing things, and all the time he moved so each side could see how prodigious his talent was.

Still Cazaux was not impressed; such kids had been around before, had come and gone, but had never made it as footballers. But his informer insisted: this *negrito* is something else, you must come and see. The word *negrito* is important. In Argentina it means someone from the social margins, from the shanty towns beyond the city, with Bolivian or Paraguayan blood, perhaps with Indian blood, but with darker skin than the ruling class. That was the word Cazaux first heard to describe Maradona.

Eventually, he went to see him and he loved him. He still remembers the way Maradona dominated the ball, he still remembers his speed. He knew he was watching a great player. He contacted him, invited him to come to his office to accept a pair of shoes. Maradona came in with his two younger brothers in an old Fiat 1600. They were shy, but watchful, and they were well-dressed, Cazaux remembers.

It was the first time he had given shoes to such a young player. But the following year, as he watched Maradona's progress, he decided to contact him and arranged to meet him at the Sheraton Hotel. Maradona and his 'representative' came looking for sportswear, and were very surprised when they were offered a contract from Puma for fifty thousand dollars over four years. They signed.

The representative, the pudgy one (Cazaux refers to him as *el gordito*), was to stay with Maradona as agent, friend and constant companion over the next ten years. He was to become Maradona's shadow. In 1980, they sent a joint Christmas card. They were like complete opposites: Maradona was talkative, Jorge Cyterszpiler (pronounced Seeterspeeler) was taciturn, much given to monosyllabic communication; Maradona was Catholic, of Italian origin; Cyterszpiler was Jewish, of Polish origin: Cyterszpiler's older brother, his hero as a child, had been a player with Argentinos Juniors, but he had died. For a few years as an adolescent, Cyterszpiler did not go near a pitch.

He was twelve, two years older than Maradona, when they first met. Cyterszpiler had become interested in an under-age team called Los Cebollitas – the little onions – in which Maradona played. Most of the kids lived in the shanty towns outside the city and had to travel long distances for games and practices. Some, including Maradona who lived miles out in a place called Fiorito, began to stay over on Friday and Saturday nights in Cyterszpiler's house, close to the Argentinos Juniors football grounds.

Oswaldo Lopez, a Juniors official, remembers Maradona hanging around the fringes of the club from the age of eight, first as a ball-boy, then as a half-time performer and a member of Los Cebollitas. He remembers his playing style from the beginning as being without fear, without caution. No one else from Los Cebollitas ever made it into professional football,

Lopez says, but it was clear that as soon as Maradona came of age he would be taken on by Argentinos Juniors.

Maradona's first contract was negotiated by Cyterszpiler, who demanded something which the Juniors had never given to a player, and have not since: a rented apartment near the grounds for Maradona and his family. So, at fifteen, Maradona was able to take his family out of the *villa miseria* of Fiorito and house them in a modest apartment near the centre of Buenos Aires.

Later, as his fame grew and his playing became more skilled, the club bought him and his family a house. His aim, he said, was to make enough money so that his father, who worked long hours in a mill for very little money, could give up his job. Cyterszpiler remembers that when Maradona was eighteen – in 1978 – he was making enough money to support his parents and most of his seven brothers and sisters.

That was the year of the World Cup in Argentina, and Maradona was bitterly disappointed to be one of the three dropped at the last minute by Cesar Menotti. He cried like a child, Cyterszpiler says. Juan Carlos Cazaux remembers his going outside on the day he heard the news and spending more than an hour with his elbows leaning on a fence, staring into the distance. He went over it in interview after interview, how he could never forgive Menotti. But his non-inclusion was an issue only for those who closely followed sport in Argentina; his status as national hero came about only the following year when he played in the Junior World Championship in Japan, and the entire country followed his playing on television.

From then on, he was public property; everyone who came across him in the subsequent years talks about how hard it was for him, so outgoing and extrovert but unable to walk the streets without being hassled for autographs. Sergio Batista talks about Maradona's acute consciousness now that he never had a youth, that from the age of nineteen he could never go anywhere without being noticed.

He began to give constant interviews and to keep a diary, which was published in *El Grafico*. In it, he portrayed himself as a small, innocent angel, protected by Menotti and Cysterszpiler, a youngster who trained hard, did what he was told and went to bed early at night. Over and over, he talked about his family, some of whom travelled with him wherever he went. When he scored a goal, he said, he thought of his mother. When he was away, he telephoned home all the time. In 1976, after his move from Fiorito, he met Claudia Villafane and he wrote about how much he missed her when he was away.

He had no difficulty talking about his need for prayer, his love of his family or about how he cried after a match. He was, in the publicity surrounding him during his early years, goodness personified. He also began to portray himself as a victim and with good reason. He was so fast and inventive as a player that it was almost impossible to mark him. So players began to kick him. Kicking Maradona seemed to have become as much a part of the games in which he played as kicking the ball. 'All my rivals want to kick me,' he said.

During his trip to Ireland in 1980, he wrote in his diary not about the quality of the game, but about his fear that he would be kicked, and he records one particular kick from an Irish international. His performance against England at Wembley in 1980 was triumphant, and the report in *The Sunday Times* was reproduced in the Argentinian Press: 'Maradona kept possession of the ball for two minutes and ten seconds of continuous action,' it said.

Argentinians are obsessed with the view the outside world has of them, and Maradona's success abroad, especially at Wembley ('the home of football', he recorded in his diary), increased his hero status in an Argentina that was becoming

known in the outside world for illegal detentions, disappearances and an ugly military regime.

From 1980 onwards, the talk was of Europe, and of which
club would buy Maradona. By now, he had transferred from
Argentinos Juniors to Boca, another local club. There were
dark complaints in the Argentinian Press about their best
players leaving, and hope was expressed that something could
be done to keep Maradona. But he was ready to go to the
highest bidder, and so in 1982 he left Argentina to play for
Barcelona. His best years were to be spent outside Argentina.

They ask you again and again: what do you think of Argentina? Do people in Europe think this is a banana republic?
They feel abandoned by the world outside; they are, they
keep telling you, Europeans; they built Buenos Aires to look
like a European city; they are not South Americans; they
never intermarried with the natives; why, look around you,
there are no natives. (They murdered all the natives in the last
years of the nineteenth century.)

There is a sadness and a despair in the way they appeal to
you to understand them and accept them. Look at the opera
house, the Teatro Colon; all the great singers came here, they
tell you – Caruso, Galli-Curci, Joan Sutherland. They have
the list at their fingertips. This was one of the richest countries
in the world.

The great plain of Argentina was, even in the nineteenth
century, a vast emptiness. The early Spanish settlers were
looking for gold and silver, so they left the plain, the pampas,
pure clay, to the natives. Until the first half of the nineteenth
century, you could go and claim some of the richest land in
the world.

At first, Argentina thrived by exporting wheat to Europe,
but the county's real wealth came with the refrigerated ship.
They produced the best beef in the world, and they built

their capital city and their great pride out of the money they made from beef. In the last years of the nineteenth century and the first decades of the twentieth, they built mansions throughout Buenos Aires. But they never believed in Argentina and they invested their money elsewhere. They honeymooned and holidayed in Europe; they imported European furniture and fittings. Argentina was a cultural and spiritual exile.

The second wave of immigrants, from the south of Italy and northern Spain, came to service the new wealth, as labourers in the port, the mills and the slaughterhouses. They found work, but they found, too, that the wealth of the new country had already been divided up. Their sharp sense of exclusion would later take root in the Peronist movement once they had settled.

As the century progressed, the country's fabulous wealth began to evaporate. It had allowed too many outside interests to control its infrastructure. It had nothing to fall back on once Europe and the US adopted protectionist policies, nowhere else to send its beef and wheat and nothing else to send. It was destined to dream of former greatness, to grow old reminiscing about a glory turned to dust.

If you drive out from Bueno Aires to Fiorito in search of the house where Maradona was born, you move from that world of privilege and wealth and dreams to another world made up of immigrants who never shared in the wealth. You move from the planned centre of the city, with its long boulevards and expensive shops, to a township with unpaved roads and windowless shacks.

But it is not simply the contrast in architecture or streetscape that is striking. The people look different: some have Indian features, but most have darker skin, the skin of people who have been out in the sun. This is where the *negritos* live.

In Buenos Aires, people are dismissive about Fiorito: they

talk about its inhabitants in racist terms and mention Maradona's Fiorito background as signalling a sort of reduced moral and intellectual fibre. Although Sergio Batista expresses his delight at Maradona's wealth because he has come from such lowly origins, most feel that someone who comes from Fiorito cannot properly represent Argentina.

You turn off a road full of potholes on to a dirt road. Not all the people are badly dressed, but most look poor. All the houses are small, but some have been plastered and painted. There are mongrel dogs and horses everywhere. After a while there are no cars, and people sit outside the houses, staring at you as you pass. Everyone you ask can direct you to the house where Maradona was born, but the football pitch where he played as a child has been built on.

Maradona's house in Calle Azamor is big by Fiorito's standards; it is plastered and there is a window on each side of the door; there is a small yard in front, and a gate leading to the unpaved road. Its current owners are not at home, according to a young man two doors away. Yes, he says, like everyone else in the street he knew the family, he played football with Diego, but he doesn't want his name written down; everyone around here played football together. Diego's father was his godfather, he says and he knows he could go and see them any time, but, he shrugs, he sees no reason to do so, they have moved away.

Journalists have come before, he says, and been told by a group of people who gathered on the corner that Maradona used to collect scraps and cardboard when he was a child, but that simply is not true. Maradona went to school, and in Fiorito that was important. Also, this street is a settled community, unlike other parts of Fiorito where people come and go. The young man thinks these distinctions important.

Maradona has not been back to Fiorito for five or six years, the man says. The last time he came with a friend, a singer, to play in a celebrity match, but the people couldn't leave him alone, couldn't stop coming up to him and wanting to touch him. It was clear he was exasperated and would not be in a hurry to come back. People from the street were not invited to his wedding in 1989.

There is still a football pitch close to the house, close, too, to a smouldering dump. The pitch has a clay surface, perfectly laid out and flattened. It is Saturday afternoon, and there is a match in progress. The players are young, but the game is being conducted with extraordinary speed, seriousness and ferocity. All of the players are decked out in decent sports gear, despite the poverty of the locality.

Football in Argentina comes from poverty. This is the world from which Maradona and most other Argentinian professional footballers come, the world he constantly refers to, the place where he was formed. When asked if he had ever been there, a senior figure in Argentina's football organization winced and pointed to his clothes and body and said of course he had never been there; he was from Buenos Aires.

Someone from out there could never become a gentleman. 'Look at Pele,' a member of the old Argentinian bourgeoisie said. 'He came to Punte del Este [the posh seaside resort in Uruguay] last year and sat close to me in a restaurant. He was a gentleman [*un caballero*]. You could never imagine Maradona in such a place.'

The boy from Fiorito did not grow up to become a gentleman. He made no effort to join the bourgeoisie of Buenos Aires, he remained intensely loyal to his family and his childhood sweetheart and the friends he made when he moved out of Fiorito into the city. Even the house he bought for his parents in Calle Cantilo stands out in the street of quiet, detached houses as shiny and ostentatious.

His wedding was, in the words of one member of the

establishment, perhaps the most vulgar occasion ever held in Argentina. He invited more than a thousand people, flying a plane-load from Europe. It was held in the Luna Park and cost more than a million dollars. People who were there, such as Oswaldo Lopez from Argentinos Juniors or Daniel Arcacce from *El Grafico* magazine, had a great time, loved the glitter of the occasion and point out that Maradona could have had the whole event sponsored, but he chose to pay for everything himself.

Maradona had been going out with Claudia for fourteen years. When asked why he was getting married, he said he wanted to have a party, a really big one, and anyway his girlfriend's mother was being asked all the time why her daughter wasn't getting married, and he thought he should do the decent thing. He treated the whole thing as a joke.

His first child had been born two years previously, and the journalist Carlos Bonelli was invited to the huge party in the Harrods salon in the centre of Buenos Aires. Maradona led his baby daughter into the ceremony in a supermarket trolley. Antics like that, and the fact that Maradona was the best-known Argentinian in the world, were an even further humiliation for the rich of the city as inflation increased at home and the value of their investments abroad lessened each year.

But the parties and the ostentatious wealth did not help Maradona's popularity among the class he came from. He loved being photographed with stars and famous people. His visits to Buenos Aires were becoming vast media events. In the beginning, he had come to represent the outsiders in Argentina, just as General Perón had done, but as he moved towards his thirtieth birthday his fame and his wealth had placed him outside the world that produced him.

Even now, after all this time, Jorge Cyterszpiler grimaces when he hears the Catalan language spoken by the management and most supporters of the Barcelona football team. The two years Maradona spent in Barcelona were not easy. The Catalans may cheer at a football match on Sunday and passionately support their team, but the rest of the week they work hard and stick to themselves.

Maradona brought with him hangers-on, the 'clan Maradona', who peopled the nightclubs and fast-lane scene in the city. Barcelona has a reputation for nightclubs and fancy bars, but there is a strict code of laid-back, European behaviour. So a bunch of failed Argentinian footballers with nothing to do all day stuck out in the city, and in the newspapers became known as Maradona's Indians.

The more famous Maradona grew, the worse the physical attacks on him became. In Argentina before he left, the other players had begun to abuse him verbally as they marked him, taunting him for being worth millions of dollars. He did not learn to retaliate to physical attacks, unlike Pele, who was not such easy prey. 'I can't learn,' he said, when asked if he was going to start defending himself. He also remarked that so much attention was paid to his behaviour on the pitch that if he elbowed an opponent it would be photographed and seen all over the world.

The most famous attack on him was in Barcelona in January 1984 when a Basque opponent, Goicoechea, gave him a vicious kick that severed a ligament in his ankle and caused him to have thirty stitches, putting him out of action for four months.

By the end of 1983, Maradona was known to be having personal problems with the club, which sees itself as a symbol for the Catalan nation, and in 1984 he agreed to transfer to Naples.

He had felt uncomfortable in Barcelona, Jorge Cyterszpiler says, but he was not prepared for Naples. The Catalans tend to be very reticent; Maradona was not mobbed in the streets of Barcelona, and his house in the Pedralbes district offered him a good deal of privacy. Buenos Aires is a huge city with sprawling suburbs, and there are, Cyterszpiler points out, at least a hundred restaurants Maradona could go to. Naples, on the other hand, is tiny. That was Maradona's first Neapolitan shock: there were only ten restaurants to visit.

And the people did not have the natural reticence of the Catalans. Maradona was public property. He made his coming to Naples into a sort of homecoming. 'I want to make myself into the idol of the kids of Naples,' he said, 'as I was to the kids of Buenos Aires.' He loved the adulation and the openness, but soon he and Cyterszpiler realized that he would have no privacy in the city.

He was now worth a great deal of money, but was subsequently to tell an interviewer that at the age of twenty-five, around the time when he began playing for Naples, he hadn't got a penny. Cyterszpiler denies this, and says that one report has been quoted over and over. He adds that Maradona has recently told him that he never said he was broke at twenty-five. And yet it does seem that certain foolish invest-ments were made. The Argentinian journalist Carlos Bonelli did not believe that Maradona had invested money in the bingo business in Paraguay until he was in Asunción himself and saw a Maradona bingo hall in the most exclusive suburb of the city, two blocks away from where Somoza was assassi-nated and close to where government ministers were living. It was not doing good business.

In 1985, Maradona and Cyterszpiler split up in acrimony. Cyterszpiler went back to Argentina, and Maradona's new manager, Guillermo Cuppola, did not encourage Maradona to see him again. Cyterszpiler was not one of the thousand friends invited to Maradona's wedding in 1989. He dedicated himself, back in the old country, to furthering the career of

92

an obscure Peronist politician called Carlos Menem and became chief of his campaign organization during the presidential elections, which Menem won. ('I'm thirty-two,' he says proudly, 'and I've managed Maradona and Menem.')

Cuppola was the exact opposite to Cyterszpiler. It would be almost impossible to imagine Cyterszpiler in a nightclub; Cuppola loved nightclubs; he was talkative, outgoing, he enjoyed the high life. He had been married to an actress and he liked being photographed with beautiful women. He had started from the bottom, as a messenger boy in a bank. He had begun to work on the side as a players' agent, and at one point he had almost two hundred Argentinian players and managers on his books.

Cuppola devoted his entire time to Maradona's career. He was now the most expensive player in the world, and Cuppola, it is said, handled his finances with great skill. But as Maradona changed the fortunes of his club, Naples itself became more and more of a nightmare. He was a prisoner in his apartment. Carlos Bilardo, the manager of the Argentinian football team from 1983 to 1990, says the effect on Maradona should not be underestimated. He couldn't go out on the street, Bilardo says, and if he was asked to sign an autograph and refused, news would spread that Maradona had insulted a fan.

On tour, Bilardo says, Maradona couldn't even go down to the hotel lobby. If the rest of the team went to a restaurant with Maradona, they knew their meal would be constantly interrupted, so Maradona tended not to go out with them.

Opponents continued to kick him. Puma's Cazaux spoke to a doctor who had seen him after a match and remarked that his body was covered in bruises. In his seven seasons with Napoli, the club won two Italian titles, one UEFA Cup and one Italian Cup. In Maradona's first season alone, the club easily recouped his purchase price by increased ticket sales. He was treated like royalty as long as he continued to deliver.

But every move he made was subjected to scrutiny. A woman claimed he was the father of her child. There were other claims that he was seeing unsavoury people and hiring prostitutes. The problem for him and for Cuppola was when and how to leave Naples. Clearly, in retrospect, had he left in 1990, he would have become a great myth and a hero in Naples, but his contract demanded that he stay on, so he stayed.

Last November, for reasons that have never been explained, Cuppola retired as his manager – he has since denied in the magazine *Somos* that he ever saw Maradona taking cocaine – and so Maradona was left in Naples between then and April without an essential piece of his protection. Once he ceased to deliver, once his erratic behaviour became a hindrance to Napoli's (his team) fortunes, he was defenceless in the city. It would be easy to make him a scapegoat. He lacked the guile and watchfulness to save himself.

Last November, Maradona refused to travel with Napoli to Moscow for a European Championship game. He made no secret of the fact that he had been out the previous night having a good time. Napoli were eliminated from the tournament, which cost the club a great deal of money in potential ticket sales. A few months later, Maradona was subjected to a cocaine test, which he failed, and suspended from soccer for fifteen months by FIFA, the world soccer association.

There is a terrible sadness about Buenos Aires now. Its glory has departed; the great singers no longer come to the Teatro Colon: all the cars are old.

Everything has been tried to get the economy working again. In the 1970s, the generals who took over from Isabel Perón decided to borrow money to keep the value of the currency artificially high. They hoped Argentinian industry would import machinery at low cost. Instead, the Argentinians, on discovering their pesos were worth a fortune outside Argentina, began to travel. They bought anything they could lay their hands on in France, in Spain, in the US. Taxi drivers, it is said, could afford to take their holidays in Tokyo.

This period is now referred to as *la época de la plata dulce*, the years of the sweet money, and it did not last long. It was to become the Indian summer of the Argentinian dream. They are still paying back the money. It was in Europe and the US that they first heard of the disappearances, how people were being picked up by the police and the army and never seen again, and this was happening in their own country. Many of them still do not believe it ever happened, although there are at least ten thousand names unaccounted for.

They are proud of Argentina, they love its flag and its national anthem. They were outraged when the Italians booed the anthem during the 1990 World Cup. They are loyal to the army, whose generals are members of the old aristocracy, and so the defeat in the Falklands War is an unmentionable event, a trauma that has not yet been exorcized.

For ordinary people, democracy means you can feel free to say what you please, and that is good. Except what people say is that wages are not keeping up with massive inflation, that you need two jobs to live and that there is no sign that things are going to improve. In 1985, the peso was replaced by the austral; now the austral has become debased.

The presidency of Raúl Alfonsín, who took over from the generals in 1983, was a period of great industrial strife, which often crippled Buenos Aires and did not help the Argentinian economy. But at least Alfonsín was an honest and stabilizing influence. His successor, Carlos Menem, the obscure politician whom Jorge Cyterszpiler helped to power, the man who made Maradona Argentina's ambassador for sport, has provided Argentina with a soap opera that may have amused the outside world but has done nothing for Argentina's great pride.

His difficult relationship with his wife, their public rows, her eviction from the presidential palace became part of the daily news in his first year. Since then, the allegations against Menem and his wife and his wife's family have become more serious. They include the accusation that Menem's sister-in-law carried suitcases of drug money – each said to contain a million dollars – into Argentina and was let through customs at the airport in Buenos Aires by her ex-husband, an airport official. Argentina's Vice-President, Eduardo Duhalde, remarked that Menem's wife's family 'are making the government look like a situation-comedy show'.

The Argentinians' nightmare is that people all over the world will laugh at them. Menem is one aspect of their shame; now Diego Maradona is back in the city in disgrace, after admitting that over the past three years he has been taking cocaine. He is seeing psychiatrists and keeping a low profile. Recently, while out running in the suburbs, he met a group of joggers. He said he would run with them as long as they did not ask him to talk. His lawyers have made it clear he must say nothing.

Jorge Cyterszpiler has begun to see him again, after a break of more than five years. Sergio Batista has missed practice with his team to go and train with Maradona, who has a private football pitch and sports complex outside the city. He is living quietly, Batista says, and, more than anything else, he feels shame for what he has done.

People speak well of him now that he is back. Carlos Bilardo speaks of him as the most perfect and well-behaved player he has ever known. For the many companies who have sponsored him, it is vital that his reputation be salvaged in some way, that the parties, cocaine and women are seen as a thing of the past.

His family still adores him. His photograph has pride of place in the hallway of his parents' house. The journalist Carlos Bonelli accompanied him on a trip to Cuba several years ago with members of his family, including his mother and two sisters. He remembers how Maradona basked in their adulation. He loves being loved.

On that trip to Cuba, Bonelli remembers Maradona on the beach, how he could not sit still, how he played all day with a football, tossing it in the air, running with it. He can't stop performing. Carlos Bilardo believes that he will play again, and Sergio Batista hopes that he will. But over the past few weeks, Batista says, Maradona himself has been insisting he will not return to the game, that he is ready now to begin to live and wants to retire from football.

Most observers in Buenos Aires agree he will not be sent to jail, if he is convicted as a result of the April 26 raid, but be given some sort of suspended sentence. It will be hard for him, Batista says, to settle down after all the adulation, all the fame and glory. 'It's very difficult,' Batista says. 'He lost his youth. He didn't have a youth. He says he doesn't want to play again.'

1991

The Afterlife

PAUL MORLEY

Suddenly, grown men sigh.

They can't help it. They're watching a video compilation of the sporting life and social adventures of George Best in a small theatre at a Bristol hotel. On the screen, the swift and beautiful twenty-year-old George Best is creating, out of next to nothing, the second of the two goals he scored in a 1966 European Cup game against the invincible Benfica in front of 75,000 of their own fans. There's a kind of hush in the darkened theatre as Best begins a run everyone knows can only end in triumph.

What happens next is so brilliant and so fresh that the people in the theatre can scarcely control themselves. It's seven seconds of natural white magic produced by a crazy young fool who could do things with a football that amounted to an extravagant assault on reality's cautious grind. He blinds a troop of Benfica defenders with lightness of touch, slips right through them as if they were air, then strokes the ball past the goalkeeper. A complex plot of movement and mystery is over in a flash. Twenty-five years later, in the dark, grown men sigh as one, intimately, involuntarily. You might have seen this goal a hundred times before, but watching it come alive again is still sexy, and it still exists in the present. It is a goal good enough to produce a change in the weather.

A few minutes later, the chunky and dishevelled forty-five-year-old George Best is amusing the invited audience with tarted-up tall tales of how amazing he was: at football, at fucking, at drinking, at just plain Irish living. The video they have just watched was called *Genius*, and they listen and laugh as the ghost of a genius spends a little more of his time coming to terms with his past. He remembers that second goal against Benfica so vividly it's as if it hadn't happened yet, as if it was just a fantasy, a goal he was imagining he could score.

'If I'd have scored a third,' he cheerfully brags, as if he's well aware that the flying, craving young man who scored that goal is only dreamily connected to the saucy, frivolous middle-aged man who remembers the brilliant ease of scoring it, 'then I would have walked off the pitch.'

Manchester United beat Benfica 5–1 that night. Best flew back into London after the game with a new nickname, El Beatle, and the kind of fame that would both make his life and spoil his life, a fame that he could hear, ticking next to his ear like a bomb about to go off, a momentum that became his existence. Before those two goals in Benfica he was a famous footballer who was cute enough and unpredictable enough to be getting some pop-teen publicity. He arrived back in London as a successful living display of fashionable long hair and boutique clothes, boasting the cracking confidence and hedonistic smile that saw him easily manipulated as a star feature of the overheated Sixties. On the front page of the *Daily Mirror* the day after he arrived there was a photograph taken from behind of someone wearing a flamboyant sombrero and a flash leather coat. 'WHO IS THIS?' demanded the headline. The answer was on the back page, the sports page. It wasn't a pop star, or a fashion designer, or an actor.

'It was *me*!' Even now, Best seems a little alarmed. 'I

remember thinking at the time – the front page *and* the back page of a national newspaper. I don't think it had happened before, and it hasn't happened much since. That's when I knew it was starting to become a monster. I was put in a goldfish bowl. It's been like that ever since. For twenty-five years . . .'

'A beer, please.

The man behind the bar at the San Lorenzo looks at me as if I have just insulted his mother and skinned his pet cat. It seems that you are not meant simply to ask for a drink in the bar of this recession-resistant, double-chic Knightsbridge restaurant. If you are a first-time visitor, you must announce your presence, or the name of the person you are meeting. It's not a place where you can just walk off the street and ask for a beer, please. Inside the restaurant, people with power at their fingertips are beginning their lunches, and as I wait at the bar, confident, well-dressed lovers and winners are arriving to eat their smart comforting meals.

A few moments later, I am with George Best, who is visiting one of his favourite places, somewhere he can forget the goldfish bowl for a couple of hours and approximately enjoy the sunshine of well-being. People will come up to him and ask for bits of paper to be signed, offer their best wishes, but in an affectionate, unthreatening way. We move to our table, begin a bottle of wine, and talk about the things George Best always seems to talk about – starting with himself and ending with himself – a few tables away from where the Princess of Wales and her friends are eating lunch. The atmosphere in the restaurant is cool and protective, and it's as if we're quietly celebrating the sweet, twisting, ego-inflating comforts of twenty-five years of hard, fast fame.

There are times during the burlesque psychodrama of being George Best when he is *up*. And when George Best is up, he's very, very up. His eyes shine and his smile is dead appealing and you catch a glimpse of the fickle cockiness that was part of the precious mixture it was simple to call genius. Sometimes, if you don't think too hard about it, you might even think that life has been kind to George Best, that he has had it all, and he can handle not having it all. That he's in control of himself, that he can cope with being the ghost of a genius, the wizard that was, drifting and shunting through a dream world stripped of his magic powers.

'The privileges of being George Best,' he decides at the San Lorenzo (although he might change his mind later, because frankly nothing in his dream world is particularly consecutive), 'far outweigh the disadvantages, by a long way. It's given me access to a fantastic world, and over the years I've had the respect of some great artists. I get on well with famous people, they've gone through what I've gone through, so I don't have to explain to them what it's all about, that sometimes I just can't help some of the things I do that look weak and selfish to the outside world. Ordinary people . . .' Best stutters as he says this, but he can't find a better way to say it '. . . can have no idea of the pressure there can be. Some great people have done some things for me out of the blue that have freaked me out. Eric Clapton came to see me once when I was having a bad time, just to say hello, have a cup of tea. We chatted for hours like a couple of old pals. It was lovely.

'Things like that, you can't put a price on. It's like, I can go to 10 Downing Street, where I've been the guest of the Prime Minister – not this one, when I was younger – and the night before, I went down the pub with the boys. I felt just as at home doing either. All my life seems to be a case of total opposites. There are no in-betweens. I live a life of absolute extremes, one day being with high fliers, the next day down the local. Someone told me that it's a trait of the Irish – living all sorts of extremes on a daily basis. One minute I feel like a million dollars, the next minute I think it's the end of the world.'

When George Best is down, he's very, very down. The gleam in his eye disintegrates. He is shattered by the volatile conditions of his fame, wiped out by decades of addiction, passions and recriminations. His life is no longer the ultimate freelance adventure, it is a grim, disillusioning search for pertinence and courtesy. When's he up, it's as though he can almost claim what he craves, a kind of mythic dignity, a deep, constant respect. When he's down, an incoherent, brittle truth stabs him in the heart: he's a sullen, drunken, aimless has-been who spiteful, all-time no-hopers are out to get. With George Best there is no such thing as *the* truth, just a tangle of could-be truths and would-be truths and things that happen most days of his life that are kind of unbelievable.

'You hear about me getting in fights ... Every time I go out there are about half a dozen situations that could get nasty. Most of the time I'll laugh it off or someone will take care of it for me, cool it down. Occasionally, I have enough, and I lash out ... and you hear about that. You never hear about the people who hit me over the head with pint pots or beat me up on the street just because of who I am. One guy in a pub split my skull in three places. When the police asked him why he did it, he said because I never played for Liverpool. He got a three-month suspended sentence. I had headaches for years afterwards.'

One week after we've enjoyed a peaceful, prosperous lunch at the San Lorenzo, George Best is in court on a charge of simple assault. As his cab pulls up outside London's Marylebone Magistrates Court, a grubby scrum of journalists and cameramen scuffle towards it, complacently determined to make a corny fuss over Best's current silly plight. When he climbs out of the cab, tape recorders and cameras are inches away from his face. It's a face that's dead to this world, a face that belongs in someone else's dream world, an opaque, frozen face that even so gives away Best's exhausted thoughts. He thinks that there is no way on earth he should be here, harassed by carelessly intrusive tabloid journalists, once again pushed up against the superficial realities of his pitiable brawling, boozing image, forced to deal with it or deny it or change so much that he's not even himself any more, made to do the thing he hates doing most, to take orders, to be reasonable, to be responsible. All because once upon a time he could do things with a football that could invade your dreams. He thinks he's being punished because he was the best, and he boasted about it, and you don't do that in this country. Or perhaps he's hunted after all these years because he wasted his talent, ran away from it, turned an embarrassment of riches into unadorned embarrassment, let open magic dissolve into wearying self-pity.

He breaks away from the journalists, telling them nothing, because how could he begin to tell them how betrayed he feels, how envied, how frustrated and how foolish? Wrapped up in himself, he doesn't even know himself, because he's always changing. In court, we are going to see one of the many George Bests, the remote, persecuted George Best, which is as real as any of them.

'During a twenty-four-hour period,' he will tell me, giving me a clue as to how hard it is to get a clue about what makes George Best something like he is, 'there will perhaps be an hour where I am anything like the popular image that there is of me. During the other twenty-three hours, I'm many other things.'

Looking for another clue, I ask Best about self-pity, how his response to his unique quandary can often seep into bitterness.

'I get depressed, and I take it out on myself,' he begins. Often when I'm asking him a question, I'm not quite sure if he's heard it properly, or whether he's heard it only too well and is dummying past it. He has a way of neatly swerving around a direct question: not backing away or staggering to one side, but sort of pushing the question between your legs, prancing past you, and abstractly accelerating off into the distance of his own exiled logic.

'I don't have sour grapes about anything. I've had a great life. I've still got a great life. I've got no reason to be sour about anything. And if things do get bad, there's always another day. I think if there is any self-pity, it's purely and simply from the footballing side, because I didn't want it to end the way it did. I wanted it to carry on longer than it did. Sure, I can feel sorry for myself. A lot of things have gone wrong for me, and I did stop playing football at the highest level when I was only twenty-six. You know, I used to kid myself when I finished at Manchester United, say to myself that it didn't matter. But it did. I'd done something I'd loved doing, at the very highest level possible, with the greatest players in the world. Who wouldn't miss that?'

Did the United years pass very quickly?

'Oh God, yeah ... It seems like two minutes, thinking about it. And when I think what I packed into those two minutes, it's amazing. If someone had written a script about what happened to me between the ages of fifteen and twenty-six, no one would believe it. Impossible. A fairy story. But it happened. It all happened. From day one – leaving home in Belfast, and then it was non-stop.'

Best arrived at Manchester United an undersized teenager with an accent that no one could understand. He ran back home after just a day of sickness and confusion in the new big city. He still has those fifteen-year-old emotions, now matched with an accumulation of devious, resilient, mock-adult skills that help and hinder him in dealing with the claustrophobia of his dream life. One way of seeing George Best is to see a combination of aggressive childishness and primitive wisdom. Until it all changes.

'It was really lucky that my dad sent me straight back to Manchester after I ran away, and that Sir Matt Busby took me back. I mean, I ran away from the top club in the country! It was madness. I could have ended up staying in Belfast, playing Irish League football, having a regular job. I would have been a caged animal. Those years at Manchester United did give me enough freedom to be myself.'

And have you spent the rest of your life recovering?

'Maybe so . . .' He slips the question through my legs. 'But really at the end of the day I think I've handled it, considering what I've been through. I mean, separate things have gone wrong, but not the whole thing. To survive has been a kind of success. There's been the early finish . . . the bankruptcy . . . the gambling . . . divorce . . . my mother's death . . . prison . . . alcoholism . . . I could have quite easily gone right down the tube . . .'

A few days before the trial, I spend a couple of days with Best at a Bristol country club hotel, where he will perform two charity events. On the second of these days it's his forty-fifth birthday, and I have dinner with Best and his partner, Mary Shatila, an hour before the show.

It is fair and unfair to say that Best is an uncompromising, contrary, self-centred man who lives for and against himself, as much as he has generous intentions and is devoted to his family. Sometimes, you're tempted to forgive him for being so bloody-minded. Whatever it mysteriously was that made him a more explosive and irrepressible footballer than just about anyone else, now makes him more dogmatic and more arrogant and more easily aggravated than just about anyone else. The touchiness and unforgiving selfishness that made him such an unpredictable, flamboyant player haven't drained away just because now there's basically nothing for him to do but spend his time finding ways to spend his time.

'As a player I never wanted to be mediocre. I always wanted to be different. I knew I was different. And I still feel the same. It's probably why I'll never be a goody-goody or anything like that. If somebody asks me something, I'll give them a straight answer.'

He hates anyone giving him advice or trying to help: he's prouder than just about anyone else. 'The people I respect are the people who don't give me advice. My father doesn't give me advice. He knows that if people tell me to do something, I'll do the opposite.'

Best says this with the air of someone who is long beyond pretending to analyse why he is so self-destructive: as far as he's concerned, and that's far enough, he's self-destructive and escapist for the same reasons that his eyes are watery blue and his accent supple Irish.

The hotel management send a bottle of champagne to the table and a waitress brings a birthday card that the hotel staff have signed. In the bar the other side of the restaurant, people are arriving for Best's entertainment. He hides himself behind a wooden partition, because he likes to make them think that he's not going to turn up. Sometimes, he enjoys his reputation, plays to his popular image. It's what people want, and he wants them to still want him. We drink the champagne, and he happily tells me funny stories about Van Morrison, Kenny Dalglish and Denis Law. In a few minutes he'll be doing what he loves most: entertaining people. Showing off. Living the dream life, because who knows what will happen the next day, or the next week?

The next week, a deadpan George Best will spend a miserable, edgy afternoon having the dried sadness of his life grimly caricatured in the dull, still gloom of a magistrates court. He's watched over by a mean, twitchy gallery of press creatures impatiently waiting for a description of his drunken daftness so that they can make yet more half-hearted additions to the dreary, one-sided image of Best as the bad boy.

An unemployed builder called Paul Davis has taken out a private summons against Best. The complaint concerns a bit of pushing and shoving in a lager state on the pavement outside a pub at closing time, which Davis readily admits left no marks on him.

What is disappointing is not so much that Best has again been trapped scrapping, but that the cause was a sweepstake which he had organized in a Paddington pub. What is the most scintillating footballer of his generation doing running a small-time patch of gambling based on the result of the American Football Superbowl? Asking for trouble, that's what. Ending up having to pay the winner, Davis, £200 and, apparently, avoiding him. Perhaps there's a tiny, would-be truth here: that Best needs this kind of trouble, this dismal attention, to keep up a connection with his past, his presence. At least he's noticed. Another would-be truth is that he's hating every damn dream second of the proceedings.

But Best does lay himself open so men like Davis can get the chance to take revenge on a celebrity giant. Davis has found a way to get people to pay attention to him, the way people have paid attention to Best nearly all his life. He is wearing his funeral suit, his stringy long hair is clean and brushed, and a cheap pair of aviator sunglasses hang jauntily out of his breast pocket. At last he's noticed. It's his day, and he's desperately keen to succeed, to prove his point, to be better than Best.

He announces that he is going to conduct his own defence. He blushes. '. . . er . . . prosecution'. Ratty and rattled, but greatly enjoying the drama that he has created out of a night's drinking and a small wager, Davis cross-examines Best. 'You make a habit of showing off about your fighting prowess,' he reads out in an over-prepared way.

'You mean,' Best quietly replies, avoiding eye contact, straining hard to be tolerant, 'that the press do on my behalf.' The smirking press tense a little, hoping that the two sorry opponents will forget where they are and begin their school-boy scuffle all over again.

'Who,' triumphs Davis, beginning to shake with his own sense of cunning, 'said that, "I hit Michael Caine to the floor in Tramps nightclub"?' Davis reaches a pitch of excitement: in his imagination he's just dribbled past three defenders and is about to magnificently lob the goalkeeper as 40,000 fans roar their approval. 'You did! In your book!' He pulls a copy of George Best's autobiography, *The Good, The Bad and The Bubbly*, from a carrier bag and waves it at Best, who blinks his eyes as if it is just dawning on him that all this is really happening. 'If you say you didn't hit Michael Caine,' shouts Davis, 'then you lied to a nation!'

Best looks slightly dazed at this erratic challenge, and now knows for real that he's not going to wake up. He's not sure whether to howl in protest, laugh hysterically or sob to himself. Sometimes being George Best just takes up too much of his time. The elderly magistrate inscrutably scribbles his notes, showing no signs of noticing that the minor drama in front of him is half-crazed. Davis asks Best some more questions.

Is it true that you wouldn't pay me my £200?

Did you or did you not tell me to fuck off when I asked you for my money?

Have you ever hit a policeman?

Have you ever been in prison?

Do you drink every day?

Why did you hit me?

Do you suffer from alcoholic blackouts?

As the questions pile up, George Best looks like he wants to escape. He looks as though he could do with a drink.

'Hands up,' asks Best, glass of white wine in hand, 'all of you who thought I wouldn't turn up.' The audience laugh and clap. Their Georgie Best is sharing memories, playing himself at nostalgia, reporting from the inside what it was like to go through his fated motions, remembering the goals he scored and the moves he made and the Miss Worlds he slept with and the managers he annoyed and the hangovers he had. In Bristol, Best answers a different set of questions, questions that set him up as an enduring hero, a spunky enigma with a crude common touch who's been and seen places his audience can only dream about.

Somebody asks him what he would do if he was a manager who had a George Best to look after, a twenty-year-old who didn't turn up for training, who was always disappearing.

'I'd find out where he was drinking, who he was shagging, and if he was as good as I was, then I'd let him get on with it,' is Best's reply.

Somebody else asks what he will be doing in five or six years.

'Shagging, I suppose. My life is the three Irish f's.' He pretends he's not going to tell us what they are. 'Oh, go on then. Fucking, fighting and fucking drinking. In that order.'

Why?

'Because it's the only order that I can remember.'

What's the single decision he would most like to change?

'The easy answer is leaving Manchester United. I should have stuck around while they rebuilt the team. If it had been any other manager than Tommy Docherty, I would have. But actually, the answer is – I took a penalty against Chelsea in 1971, and Peter Bonetti, the fucker, he saved it! I wish I'd sent it the other way.'

The audience's two favourite topics are Paul Gascoigne and *Wogan*.

'Gascoigne is a complete fucking nutter! We go to the same health farm – he needs it more than me! When he wears a number ten, I thought it was his position – but it turns out to be his IQ! He's a good kid and I like watching him play, but he just doesn't stop to think.'

Best's smashed appearance on *Wogan* confirmed his image as a broken legend spending his life midway through a nervous breakdown, refreshed his fame and, perversely, added to his bandy charm.

'They gave me some wine to relax before the show,' he says. 'I was relaxed all right – I was fucking pissed! The nice thing is – they want me back.' The audience applaud.

Best will later tell me that even though he didn't leave the house for three days after the show, when he did, 'People were lovely to me. They came up to me and shook my hand. It's something about the British – they're suspicious of some-one doing well, but they love to see you make a fool of yourself.'

Before and after the shows in Bristol, he's surrounded by people asking him the same questions, telling him the same things, wanting to hear the same stories. Sometimes there's a smile on his face, sometimes he's deeply pensive, occasionally he's with the people he's talking to, and then he seems to be lost in thought, lost in his dream world, putting up with his predicament, stuck with himself, but still telling tales, still listening politely.

'I can actually talk to people and look like I'm having a conversation with them, and I'm not. I can be talking to someone and be thinking something completely different. I can look them straight in the eye and they have no idea. They think I'm talking with them, and I'm a million miles away, just mouthing the words. It's a trick I've learnt over the years. Sometimes you just have to do it. I do it with friends. I do it when I'm being interviewed.'

Paul Davis is telling the court about George Best and the £200 that he was owed. 'After he told me to fuck off in the pub, I thought, I'm going to get my money. I'll catch him early the next day while he's still sober.'

This is meant to be a dig at Best, but Best isn't really in the courtroom. A dream world that he works hard at keeping simple is playing tricks on him today. Best, Davis and four witnesses to the events all have different stories. Best has claimed that he was in Manchester on the day the assault apparently happened, but has to admit that he cannot remember when he returned to London: he can't remember what day, what time, what train. The rough details of what happened were lost when everyone sobered up. Best's lawyer accuses Davis of being aggressive in his line of questioning. 'The only aggressive one here,' spits Davis, 'is Best, which I am going to prove.'

Are you taking out this prosecution only because my client is a public figure?

'He's not a public figure at all,' snarls Davis with confused contempt, immediately contradicting himself by saying. 'He thinks he can get away with it because he's George Best.'

Best sighs, as if it is still a shock to him that he is, after all, George Best. Perhaps the most interesting moment during the few hours we're all in court is when the magistrate asks what Best's occupation is.

'Soccer coach,' he replies.

The happiest I see George Best is when he is in front of an audience, a place where you can see him come alive. The saddest I see George Best is out of the corner of my eye, when he's sat in a bar, or slouched in a court, or travelling in a cab, and for a moment it seems to dawn on him that there is no solution to whatever it is he's always in the middle of.

As we travel on the InterCity back from Bristol to London, Best fills in all the quiz words in that day's tabloids. He's addicted to them, and is furious if he misses an edition of the Channel 4 quiz show *Fifteen To One*. He'll sit watching it, determined to get as many of the answers as possible. Watching him do this, and play pool or snooker, hating to lose, to come second, you can see that none of his overpowering competitive-ness has left him. 'There is no such thing as coming second,' he intones. 'There is no such thing as "just a game".'

As the third person in half an hour shakes Best's hand and tells him he was the greatest footballer they ever saw, I ask him if, after all that has happened and is happening, he hopes to grow old with some kind of dignity.

'I certainly don't want to end up getting mellow. But then I'd hate in ten or fifteen years to be seen as a grumpy old sod who's always moaning about this or that. I know in myself I can grow old in style, if other people let me.

'I suppose it all depends on when I look at my life and decide I've had enough of being here, there and everywhere. Even Chelsea isn't what I consider to be a home, where I would like to settle down. I still consider Belfast my home. But it changes every month, what I want to do.

'I was told a long time ago by a doctor, we were talking about alcohol, and he said that there'll come a time all of a sudden when you decide to leave the lights on or switch them off. He said, "Don't worry, it will take care of itself." I started being like that. I don't worry about what's going to happen tomorrow. I've become a supreme optimist, really. I always used to think the worst, but now I always believe that there is going to be something better around the corner.'

You've decided to leave the lights on?

'At the moment, yeah. I've been so close to rock bottom so many times that I've decided it's actually not going to happen. I can still make it . . .'

Eventually, there comes the moment when I buy George Best a drink. For some reason, I put the moment off for a long time, even though during the many hours I spent with Best there was never a minute he didn't have a drink in his hand. At the moment he drinks only white wine and champagne. 'It's cleaner. It does the same to my body as the vodka, but somehow . . . I feel better on it.'

I suppose I felt that if I bought Best a drink I was somehow adding to his problems, encouraging an alcoholic, tempting some weird fate. Mary has come across this reluctance many times before. 'Yeah, people are always asking me if it's all right to buy him a drink and I say, "Look, George is his own man." And anyway, if he wants a drink he'll have one.'

'Nothing is going to stop me,' murmurs Best.

Alcohol trickles through this article, it pours through George Best's life. He once spent thirty days drinking without eating. There is so much to say about George Best's drinking that really there is nothing to say. The way he drinks is so obvious, so hard and monotonous and consistent, that it becomes invisible.

He can talk about alcohol for hours and say nothing clear, nothing insightful, nothing revealing. He drinks through his waking hours and then he stops and then he starts drinking again. He has made up his own rules for dealing with it. He says, 'I am an alcoholic. It controls me more than I control it,' with absolutely no intention of stopping, as if by stopping he will disappear.

He readily admits that drink has caused all his problems, as if to say, well, if I didn't drink, things would be worse.

Somehow, he has detached himself from the person and the problems he talks about: here, he needs the drink to function, to complete himself as an individual, and over there, he impassively catalogues the wreckage. 'Cash problems . . . family problems . . . police problems . . . fight problems . . . it's ruined everything . . . it's phenomenal.'

In his show, he jokes that it was Sir Matt Busby who turned him to drink, getting him to drink a pint of Guinness a day to help him put on weight, and then one pint became ten, and then it became lager, vodka, whisky . . . He knows that this is a wicked thing to say, because he loves Busby, and often mentions how proud he was when Busby told him that Manchester United couldn't have won the European Cup without him.

But Best is at the farthest limits of his atrophied logic when it comes to talking about drink. He can power through five glasses of champagne as he describes the physical and mental punishment that he has brought on himself through alcohol, the missed opportunities, the loss of work, the shame, the pain, the self-torture, the dire necessity. He's astounded that he's come through what he's come through, but he has, and he still drinks, as if he still believes it can lead him to paradise, as if he still imagines that it can help him mimic some of the different kinds of feeling of being some kind of genius.

There isn't any answer. If there was, he would have thought of it a long time ago. The best answer is to drink some more. And as he drinks, he might get wild, or incoherent, or maudlin, he might rage against the world, but mostly he just sort of passes the time of day. And it makes his world a dream world, it softens the edges, and if they get jagged again, he starts drinking again.

'I used to worry about it, when it started to get out of hand and I tried to keep it secret. I was worried if people saw me staggering out of bars. Now, I don't give a shit. This is the way I live. It makes me feel better being open about my drink rather than trying to hide it. I don't give a toss who sees me crawling out of a bar, staggering into a cab. That's what I want to do.'

Is the drinking killing you – have you been told that you have only so much time to live?

'Yes. But I look at it stupidly. I think – so what? It's like, whose life is it anyway? The way I do it is I drink until I go to sleep and when I wake up, if I want some more I'll have some, and if I don't, I won't. And sometimes I don't. It's a disease, and it makes me feel better.

'It's wrecked my life, and I've managed to come through it, to a point. I drink, and I have to deal with the consequences. If I thought about it any more than that, I'd have to drink even more to handle it.'

Why do you drink?

'I enjoy it.'

During one intense drinking session, during which I vainly attempted to match him glass of champagne for glass of champagne, I got so drunk I felt myself slipping into Best's seductive, cruel, shimmering world. It was time to ask him the most important question. Was scoring a great goal just like fantastic sex?

'You just can't explain what it's like to score a great goal to someone who's never done it. I said years ago that if you'd given me the choice of going out and beating four men and smashing a goal in from thirty yards against Liverpool or going to bed with Miss World, it would have been a difficult choice. Luckily, I had both. It's just that you do one of those things in front of fifty thousand people.'

Are they both oddly lonely experiences?

'Whatever I do I can always find a way to be there but not there.'

★

'I find for the complainant.'

Abruptly, the magistrate announces his verdict. He has come to the conclusion that George Best did assault Paul Davis. Davis smirks in greasy triumph. He's scored. Best is bound over to keep the peace for a year. He sinks even further into himself. If his goals could make the sun shine, the paranoid scowl on his face now could make it rain for ever.

I'd asked him if he didn't deepen his predicament by spending hours in London pubs, gambling at pool, rising to the bait of drunken louts, glorifying the sillier parts of his reputation. He didn't really know what to say. When the tragic proportions of his life are measured out for him, all he wants to do is to leave, to get out, to be somewhere else.

'You know, in the end, what makes me happy is the thought that today I've got enough money in my pocket to buy myself a steak and a glass of champagne. I just want to do what I want to do.'

I watch Best and his friends, witnesses and hangers-on head off down the road. The journalists and cameramen chase after him, but one by one they lose interest. Best is surrounded by eight or nine people as they march off, but he's on his own. He's with himself: his best friend and his worst friend. He wants life so much to be easy that it just gets harder and harder.

I lose sight of him as he disappears into a pub. George Best is going to have a drink. And even though it will end in tears, even though someone could get hurt, even though it could even kill him, you think of the way his life is such a dream, and you have to think: who on earth can really blame him?

1991

The Grudge Match

MARTIN AMIS AND JULIAN BARNES

Martin Amis:

By analogy with Whirlwind White and Hurricane —
or, these days, better say Holocaust — Higgins, I am known,
in the snooker world, as Earthquake Amis. A *flair* player, one
who relies on *natural ability*, his only academy the pool halls
and borstal rec-rooms of a *misspent youth*: inconsistent, foul-
tempered, over-ambitious, graceless alike in victory and defeat,
and capable of missing *anything*. On the other hand, I do hit
the ball tremendously hard and with various violent spins. A
while ago I considered changing my snookering nickname
(which I am at complete liberty to do, because I'm the only
one who uses it), to take account of the New Weather: global
warming, and so on. I briefly became known as Ozone Amis.
But the past summer saw a reversion to the Old Weather
(cloud and warm rain: England in July, where the cricketer
casts no shadow), and somehow Earthquake has stuck.

I have thought long and hard and often, over the years,
about a suitable nickname for my opponent. Let's see. Snooker
frames with Julian last about twice as long as they do with
anybody else. His play is marked by exaggerated, even psy-
chotic caution, as if, after the slightest lapse on his part, I will
coolly rise from my chair and assemble a century clearance —

rather than a single miscued jump-shot double-kiss *in-off*. Otherwise he is persistent, deliberate, gentlemanly, and unpitying. He is at his strongest (and I am at my weakest) when only six or seven balls remain, when wariness is all. Oh, how he loves to thwart and hamper ... Blizzard Barnes, then, I quickly rejected: the temperature's right, but the agitation is way off target. The way he wears you down, the way he bleeds you white – if his name were Julian Garnes, he would have long been known as the Glacier. The appealing aptness of slow-moving natural processes led me to flirt with Geology Jules. Finally, though, because his style resembles not a force of nature so much as a medium of measurement or response (response to pressure, atmospheric pressure), I settled on something less personal: Barometer Barnes.

We used to play for money, he and I, twenty years ago. Pounds sterling changed hands, in note form – and they really mattered. A win or a loss could affect how well you lived for a day or two. I nearly always won, as I remember; and as we left the club or the hall I would make quite a show of hailing a taxi, offering to drop Julian off at the nearest tube. Then, years later, when he bought his own table (and a house big enough to put it in), and we started playing regularly, almost weekly, we wondered whether we should go on playing for money. Because the money didn't matter now, and our games were more evenly and bitterly fought, and we agreed that the rivalry shouldn't – and indeed couldn't – get any tenser. It's all a nightmare anyway.

Unlike the Barometer, who is largely faithful and wholly site-tenacious, the Earthquake puts out all over town. My casual opponents include a biographer, an entrepreneur, a political analyst, a tennis pro, a handyman, a philosopher and a hustler. All these players can make me flinch and squirm; but it's nothing compared to the complicated torment meted out by the Barometer. With him, even when I'm an inch away from clear victory, I sometimes wonder if I have *ever* suffered so. Why is this? Because we have 'contrasting styles', and go back a way and are both novelists? No. It's because there's nothing in it. We're equal. Each frame is decided by the tiniest psychological edge, by sniggering fate — by the sneer of the snooker gods who determine the rub of the green.

I prepared for the match with an early night, a breakfast rich in carbohydrates, and, later that morning, a secret visit to a local club, where, with a pensive pint of low-alc lager, I practised alone: to get the spasms out of my cueing arm, to neutralize the excitement (i.e. panic) of one's induction into the verdant six-bagged oblong. With epic nonchalance I motored north. We've each had our hot streaks, I won't deny: the whammy has changed hands many times. For a while, as Julian once accurately and hauntingly said to me, 'You now come here with fear in your heart.' But in recent weeks the whammy has been mine: just. Barometer Barnes received me calmly. He was pretending to take an interest in the Edberg–McEnroe fourth-rounder at Wimbledon, further claiming to see an encouraging paradigm in Edberg, the expressionless icicle, versus McEnroe, the scowling has-been. Of course, we hardly needed to say, as we made our way upstairs, that we were both nervous wrecks.

Our cues bespeak us — both, coincidentally, presents from our wives (pious admirers of their husbands' baizecraft). The Barometer's cue is a one-piece broadsword, the Earthquake's a two-piece rapier, which, moreover, comes in a yob-heaven black leatherette case with twin combination locks. His tip is ponderously broad, half the size of the cue-ball; mine is as slender as a sting — excellent for spins and miscues. The blinds were lowered. The gentlemen ruminatively chalked. I felt confident and self-possessed, and recovered quickly from the catastrophe of losing the toss.

MARTIN AMIS AND JULIAN BARNES

The pattern of our recent frames has been as follows. I go into the end-game (the colours) with a lead of about 30 — and then win on the black. The equivalent in tennis would be a 6–0 lead in the tie-break, and eventual victory at 19–17. This was, at least, an improvement on an earlier pattern, where I went into the end-game with a lead of about 30 — and then *lost* on the black. That's the Barometer for you: never more dangerous than when in the portals of the slaughterhouse. The man's an animal. My brain is encrusted with scar tissue from all the frames he has pinched and nicked. I can so easily fall apart ... In frame one I went into the colours, feeling completely hysterical, with a lead of about 30 — and won on the brown! 61–32. No sweat. Rack 'em.

Frame two, I say with tears of pride in my eyes, was a near duplicate, 51–14, my opponent disgustedly resigning with blue, pink and black still on the table. I was impressed. I was astounded. I hadn't relaxed or over-reached or crumbled or collapsed. I saved all that for frame three. All wobble and tremor, the Quake just wasn't making it on to the Richter Scale. His eyes now lit by a weak leer of hope, Barometer Barnes closed me out on the pink: 35–43.

Here's a little confession. Julian and I are not terribly good at snooker. But we *can* be terribly bad at it. The longest, if not the highest, break of the day was my five-baller, which scored 8 (green, yellow, three reds). There was also a 15 (me), a 13 (him) and a 12 (me). My opponent secured his frame three win, for example, by rifling in breaks of 4, 7, 6, 5 and 3. The fourth frame, though, was an all-howler affair, a series of abject calamities. The builders on the scaffolding outside must have thought that the house contained a pack of feral beasts, groaning at their captivity, their ill-treatment, their lousy food. At one point the score stood at 13–18, without a colour being potted. The only ball that seemed to find the pocket was the white, in a bad dream of *in-offs* and *in-withs* —

plus, from Julian, a world-class *in-instead*, the cue-ball struck with such prodigious unintentional sidespin that after a deadened impact it ambled on grimly into the corner bag. Altogether appropriately and ingloriously, the frame ended with the Barometer's *in-off* the black, the ball lasering in on the middle pocket at a preposterous angle. 58–46. 3–1. The taste of victory is sweet.

Actually I felt strangely subdued as I drove home. Gutted for the Barometer, no doubt. He took it like a man, which is better than I would have taken it. I would have taken it like a boy. Later, though, I felt tremendously happy and high-souled. I felt as if I had singlehandedly wrecked San Francisco. It occurred to me that all the pleasure of snooker comes either in anticipation or retrospect. On the table, everything is a falling-short, hamfisted, cross-purposed – a mortified groping. Come to think of it, the same goes for tennis, chess, poker, darts and pinball. Asked about his writing, the great Jimmy White once admitted that he wasn't much good at it, adding: 'Not much good at the reading neither. Either.' I *can* read and write, and to a high standard. As for snooker, well, to approach the televisual ideal, by which we all measure ourselves, I'd have to do nothing else for the rest of my life. Then snooker might work out and measure up, with everything going where you want it to go, at the right weight and angle. Then snooker might feel like writing.

Julian Barnes:

To prepare myself for this latest, and biggest, Grudge Match, I run through the list of my opponent's useful weaknesses: over-caution, middle-pocket anxiety, last-six-colours angst, plus a Plutonic rage whenever snookered more than once a frame. Then I soberly tick off my own failings:

defeatism, fear of the black off its spot, terror of the fourth ball in a break (not a regular terror for obvious reasons), plus a tendency to play my best only when several frames down. Finally, I admit our shared deficiency: that of not being very good at snooker. We make up for this, however, by an almost psychopathic competitiveness. My theory has always been that since Martin and I loathe losing to one another at games, this burns off any other rivalry between us. Lately, I've been wondering about this theory. Perhaps we're just as competitive professionally, merely better-mannered: perhaps beneath our relaxed admiration for one another's work lies the same rage to kill.

Our first frame is a macédoine of flukes and in-offs, a banquet of incompetence. Given that our five-frame match is likely to last anything up to six hours at our normal rate of play, I have decided to spring a new psychological tactic on Martin: I shall eat bananas throughout the match, as top tennis players do. Also, I've decided not to brush down the table or re-mark it or clean the balls: I reckon a few bad kicks and some low-lying grit on the baize will unsettle him more than they will me. The trouble is, if you're not hitting the balls anywhere near the pockets, dust is scarcely a major factor one way or the other. This frame, in which my highest break is eight (a fluked red plus follow-up black) would be too boring to describe in the mildest detail (yes, yes, he wins).

The only memorable moment comes when Martin commiserates with me over an ambitious red that squirms in and out of a pocket. This is memorable because, as all Martin's sporting opponents agree, words like 'Great shot,' 'What a winner,' and 'Oh, tough,' come reluctantly to his lips. But he knows about this tiny character flaw, and is working on it. So as my red skims the pocket, he tries very hard to say 'Bad luck'. Except that some inner grudgingness fights against full articulation. What comes out is '*ck*'. Oh well. 0–1. I eat half a banana.

Martin occasionally, and fancifully, likes to picture himself as a daredevil cuester, a flashing Jimmy White to my grinding Cliff Thorburn. The truth is that we are both trainee Eddie Charltons: slow, grim, defensive and almost joyless. (I sometimes wonder why we do it. We very rarely seem to enjoy it, and the pleasure of victory expresses itself mainly as relief from the self-loathing of defeat.) If frame one was poor, the start of frame two is even worse. It's a question of who stumbles into mediocrity first. And at this level of stressful incompetence, escape into averageness seems a matter of chance rather than will. I eat another half banana, thrash vainly at long pots, and resign when rather seriously behind. (The score? Oh, I expect Martin will remember the score.)

One thing, however, that is widely known about my snooker is that I am never more dangerous than when being profoundly humiliated. The third frame begins to go my way. Martin becomes careless, I settle for some solid red-and-colour, red-and-colour stuff. He misses a risky plant, I take on some banana, and win on the pink. Now this is more like it, this is turning into a match. What better display of character than to overturn 0–2 into 3–2?

By frame four I'm beginning to flow. I ease a few points ahead, Martin puts in a break of 12, I confidently reply with one of 13, and even before we reach the colours Martin is beginning to display the McEnroic aspect of his game that always encourages opponents. 'Story of my life,' he growls when a red declines to go into a pocket for the simple reason that he has hit it at the wrong angle. Yet somehow, unaccountably, I find myself 16 behind needing the last three colours to even the match.

Still, I fancy my chances. A smooth blue using the half-butt, a character-building cut on the pink, and then it's all down to the black. Martin seems to be missing by a distance as we joust it round the table, so after half a dozen exchanges

I go down with much confidence on a half-ball cut into the bottom left-hand pocket. Frame ball. It clips the pocket, and bounces away, but everything's all right, the black is clearly going safe. It rests sweetly against the cush. Then we both notice the white rolling at the acutest of angles towards the middle pocket. No danger, not really, I mean, you *never* get an in-off like that, practically parallel to the side cushion. The ball continues its slow but dogged motion, brakes at a patch of dust, trickles on, and mockingly drops. Gutted. 1–3. Mega-gutted. Martin says '*ck*'. Giga-gutted.

I don't think it was the bananas. After considerable reflection, a discussion of the match with a wide circle of friends, a session with a sports psychiatrist, and two calls to the Samaritans, I decide that I lost because Martin played much better than I did. Yes, that seems to be it. When push came to shove, the lad showed big-match composure. I console myself by reflecting that not only do I have a higher lifetime-best break than he does (34–30), I also hold several other table records. For instance, Most Humiliating Break: five balls for seven points (three reds and two yellows) *including* two flukes. Losing From An Unassailable Position: I once dissipated a lead of 65 points with only two reds left on the table. And finally, Most Reds Potted In A Row Without Managing To Get A Single Colour With Them: 15 over two consecutive frames. Martin had better look out. These are titles I cherish and do not intend to give up easily.

1991

The Other Code

THOMAS KENEALLY

In a way I owe my existence to Rugby League. In the Australian bush in the early 1930s, my mother-to-be was the daughter of a locomotive driver who watched her like a hawk and forbade her to go to the crasser ends of town. This was on the north coast of New South Wales, in a place called Kempsey, three hundred miles north of Sydney. Such was the reach of Rugby League: having been founded at the George Hotel in Huddersfield in 1890, it had now reached Kempsey, twelve or thirteen thousand miles distant.

Somehow she managed to attend a game of Rugby League. There was a tough little five-eighth – what you insist on calling a stand-off half – playing for Kempsey that day. My mother noticed that he threw a punch on the referee's blind side. This caused the large man who was marking him to hit him back more overtly. My father's forwards, believing this blow was unprovoked, rushed in to defend him. There was a brawl of props and hookers, second rowers and locks (back rows, I think you call them) from which my father extricated himself, standing back on the sideline wearing that universal five-eighth's look of perky innocence.

So when the Rugby League team next appeared to play basketball with the town's women's team, my mother picked my father out. There are old men still up there who say,

'Your old man was a wonderful five-eighth, but he used to come the knuckle.' With such a provenance, it was obvious that we would always be a Rugby League family. My eighty-three-year-old father, of Irish descent, still burns a candle in church to ensure the defeat of this or that team whose coach he dislikes or whose reputation he considers inflated.

In my babyhood, he had asked the great Australian centre Dave Brown to let me be photographed with an enormous stuffed lion Brown had brought back from a Kangaroo tour of Great Britain. Caressing it, I absorbed the message about who should be beaten at all cost: the English.

Rugby League came out of the north of England because a number of Yorkshire and Lancashire businessmen thought that talented lads should be compensated for time they took off from the pit or the plant. It therefore had a proletarian ethos.

It took eighteen years before the game moved officially to the appropriately proletarian environment of Australia. The first season was played in 1908. The first Australian team was South Sydney, named the Rabbitohs these days, because in the hard times of the Thirties the sand-dune dwellers of that part of the city subsisted by rabbit hunting.

The Rabbitohs were to contribute to international Rugby League one of the great full backs of any era, Clive Churchill, the Little Master, so dazzling there is even a stand named after him at the Sydney Cricket Ground. His kicking duels with the French full back Puig-Aubert were the talk of winter Monday mornings at school. The story was that Puig-Aubert would often snatch a smoke when play was downfield, and we lived in hope of catching him in such an act of Gallic braggadocio.

In my boyhood, we yearned to see the Poms defeated. On

Sydney suburban grounds we looked at teams clash, Wests and Souths, St George and Balmain, Norths and Detective Sergeant Bumper Farrell's Newtown Bluebags, and decided that this or that lock or half back would cut a swathe on heavy northern grounds in England. But then we would send our teams away, and they'd come back with no better than an honourable defeat in the Test Series. From the first touring team of 1911, featuring the great Dally Messenger, to 1963, Great Britain was supreme. Men like Jim Sullivan, McTigue, Karalius, the brilliant centre Eric Ashton and his winger Billy Boston, thwarted us. Then on a cold day at Swinton our magical centre Reg Gasnier and the Thornett brothers won the Ashes at last from Eric Ashton's Lions.

I was twenty-eight when it happened, and had spent therefore a whole youth in the shadow of the British Lions.

We were in part educated by the Poms. Their big forwards made a science of gaining the hard yards up the middle, purely as a prelude to sending the ball wide to their backs. I remember that the performance of the enormous Wigan props, Ken Gee and Frank Whitcombe, caused the people at the Sydney Cricket Ground in 1946 to cry, 'That's it. No more bloody food parcels for Britain!' Accustomed from childhood to the soggy paddocks of Ilkley, Bradford, Warrington and Wigan, the Poms could handle like a dream and moved the ball magically through many and quick hands.

But once we had digested the British skills, we took them over. The Great St George team of the 1950s and 1960s, the team that produced Gasnier and the great lock Johnny Raper (famous for having once walked through the streets of Ilkley wearing nothing but a bowler hat and a tie), was the team that introduced scientific cover defence. A growing athleticism and professionalism came into the game in Australia. From 1974 until 1988, the Poms didn't win a Test Match. We had yearned for supremacy and now had too much of it too easily.

Even nationalists such as myself began to tire of it, until the modern British revival that came unexpectedly at the Sydney Football stadium in the Third Test of 1988. They made the cure permanent by beating the Kangaroos last autumn at Wembley.

It was probably the finest game I have seen. No one had told the Poms they were meant to go quietly. Led by Ellery Hanley, they survived everything thrown at them, including a decimating individual try by Australia's Mark McGaw, and struck back within minutes. Afterwards we all said that it was good for the game that the transplant of power which had begun at the Sydney Football Stadium in our bi-centennial year had taken so robustly.

I have twice seen the Australians try to beat the Poms at Wembley. It is a long way from Kempsey, New South Wales, to Wembley. If people coming down from the North wearing British Coal Rugby League jumpers think they're travelling away from home and the event is rather special, imagine the feelings of an Australian as he goes up that long concourse to the Vatican of the inflated rubber bladder.

With a group of other Australians, I first went there in 1973, to see Graeme Langlands's Kangaroos take on the Lions before a much smaller crowd than honoured Ellery's boys last year.

The train out to Wembley was packed with the usual Antipodean detritus of Earls Court.

They sang their tribal songs:

'. . . The beer is crook and the girls all look . . .

Like you, you Pommie bastard.'

Apart from these racial insults, the atmosphere was genial, and all of us had seen enough of *our* boys to expect the best.

The Kangaroos were killed, above all by a second rower called Phil Lowe. He scored two tries that day. He would later come to Australia and play for my club, Manly-Warringah. Watching him, we all became aware that the style of play was beginning to favour forwards who could run as fast as wings or centres. As the aircraft carrier made the battleship obsolete, Phil Lowe established that the lumbering forward was about to join the mastodons in extinction.

Characteristically, we won the next two Tests. The second of the two is dear to my memory. We shouted ourselves first-class to Leeds, drank in the lounge of one of the better hotels until match time, and strolled down to Headingley in a biting wind, Eastern Australian writers and film makers.

Phil Lowe was as dangerous here as he had been at Wembley. But the great Australian five-eighth, child of English emigrants to Australia, Bobby Fulton, clinched the game. Lockwood, the Great Britain second-rower, hit him. Fulton lay on the permafrost, miming a cerebral haemorrhage. Lockwood was sent from the field. The Australian trainer came on with a bucket of water to try to revive the apparently comatose Fulton. Fulton opened one eye and said, 'You're not going to put water on me on a bloody cold day like this, are you, Alf?'

Ninety seconds later he intercepted a Great Britain pass and ran sixty-five yards to score. This served as a wonderful trigger for the crowd. They spent the remaining thirty minutes of the game yelling, 'Get home, you convict trash!' In the day's savage cold, all of us revelled perversely in the insult.

In the early 1970s, my wife and I moved out to the northern beaches of Sydney. Sydney is as big as Los Angeles, and I was now far from the two teams I liked – Wests and St George. I fell from the observance of the high rituals of Rugby League.

But gradually I began to write occasional pieces for newspapers. This led to the highest accolade possible in Rugby League other than actually playing for a good team: I began to be invited to games by the committee. I walked into the dressing room and saw Graham Eadie. I saw Max Krilich, child of Croatian migrants, and – close up – his famous nose, broken thirty-six times in the service of Manly and Australia. I saw that superb five-eighth, Ian Thompson, in the majesty of his sweat and grime. I saw the infant children of one of the finest second-rowers in the Phil Lowe tradition, Crusher Cleal, playing with their father's steaming boots.

For a number of seasons, before I began teaching at New York University and going to the Horn of Africa during the early part of the season, I was a tipster for the *Sydney Morning Herald*. I knew I had arrived in Rugby League the day I walked into a bar in the Australian snowfields and a twelve-year-old boy came up to ask me, 'Why did you pick Souths to beat Balmain?'

My greatest moment in Rugby League came much later, in 1989. Balmain, a municipality named for a swashbuckling surgeon of convicts, had come again to the Grand Final and were heavily favoured. They were playing the Canberra team from the Federal capital. All the commentators said they had no chance, except Bob Hawke the Prime Minister, who of course lived in Canberra and had to say that, and me, former tipster for the *Sydney Morning Herald* and occasional commentator and writer on the game.

On television I argued position by position why Canberra could win. They had Ricky Stewart and Mal Meninga, they had young forwards who were soon going to play for Australia. They had Gary Belcher at full back. On the morning of the game I was again interviewed, as a freak: the man who said Canberra could win.

The great Aboriginal winger, Chicka Ferguson, was on the

wing with Canberra, and in the last minutes, when Balmain had already sent their two most powerful forwards off, and when Bob Hawke was already on his way down from the VIP box to present the shield to Balmain, Chicka scored a wonderfully impossible weaving and jinking try to tie the game. There were twenty minutes of extra time played, in which a kid called Martin came on – he had never played in first grade before – and scored the clinching try for Canberra.

Later in the dressing room, everyone was suffering cramps. I saw the aging winger Chicka being rubbed down on a massage table and smoking a cigarette. My friend Roy Masters, former St George and Wests coach and a fine writer on politics and the game (which in Australia often blend into each other), took me up to the table and said, 'Chicka, you know Tom, don't you?' Chicka looked up, wincing with the exquisite pain of an extraordinary victory and said, 'I know you, mate, you fucking tipped us. Good on yer.'

I took those words down. It's my intention that they appear on my gravestone.

1991

Hats Off to Don King

MIKE LUPICA

The brownstone on the upper east side of Manhattan is quiet for now, quiet the way a subway platform is before the train comes. You know the D is on the way, you can even feel the ground shake a bit, see some light way back in the tunnel. But the train hasn't arrived yet. Don King has just left his office in another part of Manhattan.

On the table inside the front door there is a pile of books: *Hit Men*, *My Father Rudolf Hess*, *Winning Through Intimidation*, *Atlas Shrugged* and the new novel by Sidney Sheldon. His dining-area has a fax-machine and a copy machine. There is expensive sound equipment and a VCR, a Sergio Mendes tape and a video cassette of the movie *Ball of Fire*, probably one of Tyson's. There is a red velvet crown and a glass jar filled with gumdrops and a smaller jar filled with hard candy.

An elderly maid steps from the kitchen. 'He's comin',' she says. 'Somebody called a few minutes ago.' She disappears up the stairs, and the Manhattan home of Don King is quiet again. No shouting, no prison-yard rap, none of the 'nigger' talk he had given Spike Lee on an ABC documentary before the Mike Tyson–Alex Stewart fight. Maybe this home is more like a theme park than a subway station, a theme park before the gates open in the morning.

Behind King's desk, four black-and-white television screens

rity. This is no surprise. The owner of this place
ly made several fortunes in his life; he has made
.oo.

re he got into boxing, he was the numbers king of
eland. He spent three years and eleven months in jail for
manslaughter. Now, twenty years later, King is late for an
interview because he has been busy making another kind of
killing: closing out a two-hundred-million-dollar TV-deal,
taking Mike Tyson and Julio Cesar Chavez away from HBO.

A few days earlier, he told Spike Lee what a racist, oppres-
sive society we live in. 'You're a nigger when you're born
and a nigger when you die. If you make a pile of money,
you're just a rich nigger.'

The front door opens now, and the D train rumbles in.
King is shouting at his long-time matchmaker and sideman,
Al Braverman.

'Don't want any of them tellin' me about white folks, Al!'
King shouts. 'They gonna tell *me* about white folks?' He tries
a laugh, but it comes out flat. 'Shit,' he says, 'I've got a PhD
in Caucasianism.'

Don King shouts for the next two hours. It is part prison-
yard rap, and part the rap of a Baptist preacher. It is angry,
very angry, and funny, and brilliant, and completely ridiculous. He quotes Shakespeare and the Bible, and talks about
Goebbels and Cosby and Oprah and Tyson and Evander
Holyfield. Mostly he talks about Don King. He says he's been
investigated by the IRS, the CIA and Interpol.

'I beat all three!' King says. 'Not even Spiro T. Agnew can
say that!'

In 1972, he promoted a Muhammad Ali exhibition for a
black hospital in Cleveland. Ali fought four guys, two rounds
each. Then King promoted the Ali–Foreman fight in Zaire.
He was co-promoter for the 'Thrilla in Manila'.

'I watched the first Ali–Frazier fight in prison,' he ·
brag. 'And I promoted the third one.' In this brownst
now, fifteen years from Manila, after what seems like a
million big boxing promotions, I say to King: 'If this country
is as racist as you say, they'd find a way to hold you back.'

'They do,' he says. 'If I was white, I'd be on the cover of
Time, Newsweek, Life, Forbes. I'd be on every magazine that
was worth its salt; they'd have me there.'

'If you were white, you'd probably be leveraged out like
Trump.'

'No, no, I would have been too good for that. You've got
to understand, I'm dealing with these guys without a formal
education. The difference is my capability and my diligence
and my ability to persevere. I've never used my blackness as
an excuse. I've never got no fighter based on being black. My
performance is the only thing that's carried me through.

'You've been told the nigger is worthless, that he's shiftless,
lethargic and sloppy. He lies and steals. Stereotype image of
black folks. So I got me a new appraiser. An appraiser that
tells me America is a great country. If you have faith in God
and you persevere, you will overcome. So now I've
overcome.

'I've been blocked out of many deals because I'm black.
But I don't let that bother me. Everybody wants to make
money.'

King gives answers like that to the most innocent of
questions. In an age when sports figures have been conditioned
by the media to talk in perfect sound bites, he is the first rap
opera.

'What would happen if a controversial white man said the
things about blacks you said about whites?' I ask him. 'Do
you think that moves us along? Or do you think it polarizes
people even more?'

'The system has to be changed. The prevailing attitude of

subordinating, demeaning, degrading, humiliating, dehuman-
izing black people hasn't changed. I try to explain what
Hitler did, and the best way I can explain it is in my own
humble opinion ... The Jew was nothing but the nigger of
Germany. I live for the day when all people are clothed in
dignity. But to prove my point I have to symbolize it with
something dramatic enough to get people's attention. Hitler
did what the white American did over here in racism. He did
it with propaganda.'

Larry Holmes once said that Don King 'looks black, lives
white and thinks green'. Holmes is one of a number of boxers
who allege that Don King cheated them. Tim Witherspoon is
another. You can go all the way to junior welterweights like
Saoul Mamby.

In US boxing, it is illegal to be both promoter and manager,
a conflict of interest where a fighter can only lose. King's way
around this is to make his son Carl the manager. Witherspoon
has filed a federal lawsuit alleging he signed two contracts
with Carl King. The one with boxing commissions, he says,
had Carl taking thirty-three per cent commission. The other
had Carl taking fifty per cent.

Both Kings deny any impropriety in their dealings with
boxers. Of course the father does it at full shout.

'So why is Holmes mad at you?'

'He's mad at me because he has an Oedipus complex.'

'Larry Holmes is mad at you because he loves his mother?'

'No, no, Oedipus and his father. It's a parental thing. I've
done more for Larry Holmes and the Holmes family than his
father ever did. I've done more for Larry Holmes than he
could do for himself ... I taught him how to read and write.
I'm talking about sitting up at night, trying to help this
human being to elevate himself. Now we find him one of my
condemners.'

Don King is the same father figure to Mike Tyson that he says he was to Holmes. Their relationship is very good for him. He thinks the current heavyweight champ, Evander Holyfield, is a phoney. He says he should be stripped of his title for fighting George Foreman before Tyson because Tyson is the number-one contender and, in most people's minds, still the heavyweight champion of the world.

'Evander Holyfield's a nigger. He's going to be a nigger till he dies,' King says. 'If he's rich he's going to be a rich nigger, if he's poor, he's going to be a poor nigger.' In King's not so humble opinion, 'the people who like him like him 'cause he's docile. Holyfield can be controlled. "Run, Johnny. Sing, Johnny. Dance, Johnny."'

King predicts Foreman will win the title from Holyfield in April, fight 'bums' in Europe for a year or two and retire without ever giving Tyson a shot at his title. I tell him Tyson shouldn't have to wait years for another shot at the title.

'You're the most brilliant man I've run across,' he says. 'You touch my heart.'

He is one of the most remarkable figures in the history of sports. And he could have become the important black voice he desperately wants to be. Up close with King, you see the brains, you see the charm, you see the passion. Ultimately, though, you have to see the hustler in him. The man is full of anger. It is more impressive than his whole range of thought, from Hitler to the Bible. King knows how smart he is. But he wants more. He wants respect. Unfortunately, he is trapped in this wild-haired character he created for himself. No one can see past it. King understands that, and it makes him mad.

'They try to vilify me,' he says. 'They try to make me the worst motherfucker that ever lived. Make everybody think I hate people. Try to make me a racist, but that's impossible because I've never used racism to get where I'm at. You go to my office, you'd think it's a white office, that I'm a token nigger.'

King is at his best in his own courtroom, defence counsel and character witness and judge and jury all at once, asking and answering the questions, shouting down his accusers. But when all that is finished you have to ask yourself: are they *all* lying? Or is King a hypocrite, screaming about racism on one hand and preying on black fighters himself? He was supposed to be the impartial promoter of the Tyson–Douglas fight in Tokyo, but he tried to get the decision overturned in Tyson's favour as soon as the fight was over.

At two in the afternoon, I shut off the tape recorder and put it in my briefcase. King keeps shouting. I put on my sports jacket and then my overcoat. He does not acknowledge that I am leaving.

'They are trying to make the truth unbelievable and the untruth believable,' he shouts. I stand there with my coat on and my briefcase in my hand, and King shouts for another thirty minutes. There is something mesmerizing about it. I can understand how it happens, how a fighter like Witherspoon gets in the same room with him and signs his life away.

It is 2.40 in the afternoon when I get to the street. King is still shouting as I walk towards Third Avenue. I look back. A blonde woman in running clothes is staring at him as if he were a spaceship.

1991

Ireland's War on Eamon Dunphy

COLM TOIBIN

As the days went by, the news from Ireland was more and more astonishing. Everybody told me I was insane to be in Cagliari with the fans. At home, it was one big party: little old ladies had learned the intricacies of offside; when Ireland drew with England it was like the Pope's visit in the confines of your local bar. And the commentaries afterwards were magic. Men, women and children watched wide-eyed as John Giles and Eamon Dunphy, two players turned journalists, went through the match.

I went to Palermo for the Ireland–Egypt match, and still there was nothing to report. No hooligans, and no excitement either. Even the match was dull. I was sitting in my hotel room trying to compose my weekly report when the first phone call came. Had I not heard? Eamon Dunphy had become public enemy number one. At the end of the Ireland–Egypt match he had thrown down his pen with the entire nation watching, and announced that he no longer cared whether Ireland won or not, our level of playing was so bad. Whoever sent our team out to play like that should be ashamed, he said.

Within hours there were T-shirts on sale with Eamon Dunphy as the football and the Irish manager Jack Charlton, the national hero, kicking him. If this was a carnival, Dunphy was the devil.

My editor rang: he sounded low-key and hesitant. He hoped I didn't mind, he said, but he had something he wanted me to do. Eamon Dunphy was coming to Palermo to report for our paper on the Ireland–Holland match. Could I concentrate on making sure he was not molested or beaten up? In other words, I was being asked to become Dunphy's minder and bodyguard. The idea was hilarious, but I agreed none the less. Dunphy would arrive the following morning.

I knew Dunphy pretty well. He had written a column for a magazine I edited in the early 1980s. He used to arrive every Monday with his copy typed out by a typist. ('When I learn to write, I'll learn to type,' he said.) He would sit opposite me and look at me carefully as I read it. He had been a professional soccer player, leaving Dublin for Manchester United when he was fourteen. He had played one brilliant and beautiful game, he said, when Sir Matt Busby was watching and more than 40 youngsters were looking for a place as trainees. But after that, his career had been ordinary, he had played for Ireland without much success and for Millwall. By his early thirties he was back in Dublin, looking for a living.

As I read his copy on those Mondays with his eyes fixed on me, I could never understand why he thought sport was so important. He did not seem to believe that it was about winning and losing; he thought it was bigger than that. It was about moral and aesthetic issues, it was about truth. More than anything else it was about truth, absolute truth. His eyes shone with conviction, and some of his sentences too. He had taught himself to write, and the prose was clean and simple. But when he pushed himself, when he really got going about truth and beauty and football, he could write like nobody else. He could write like an angel.

Dunphy now arrived in Palermo, a man with a mission. The Irish team were playing a game which he deeply disliked; there was no beauty in what they were doing, no creativity.

The game they were playing was brutal and straightforward. The orders were to kick the ball towards the other goal and forget about fancy footwork. This, in Dunphy's view, and in the view of certain Irish players, was a travesty of what the Irish team could do with a manager other than Jack Charlton.

Ireland had fallen in love with Charlton. No journalist dared say anything against him. Only one did, and now I was his bodyguard.

The following morning there was to be a team practice followed by a press conference. Dunphy and myself, his dutiful bodyguard, stood and watched as the players got off the bus. Not one of them greeted Dunphy, even though many of them knew him and had been friendly with him. Charlton, in his book on the World Cup, described the scene: 'There was Dunphy and this little guy in a green shirt, who I later discovered was his mate, stationed in a position where they couldn't avoid being seen. Mick McCarthy taps me on the shoulder and says "Have you seen who's here?" I advised him to put on his best face and smile.'

We smiled too while the players kicked the ball around and then, with the rest of the journalists, we followed Charlton into the press centre for the press conference. Charlton's account of the event is reasonably accurate: '. . . one of the first people into the place is Dunphy. Within minutes he opens his mouth to say something. I chop him. He asks why I won't answer his questions and I tell him that I don't consider that he is a proper journalist. Whereupon the other little fellow in the green shirt [*actually, I am much taller than Dunphy*] starts complaining about my attitude. I advise him that if he wants this press conference to continue, he should take his mate outside. He refuses, so I get up and leave.'

Dunphy and I had agreed to station ourselves at opposite sides of the room, so that if Charlton refused his question or side-stepped it, then I would ask it again. Dunphy simply wanted to know if Charlton intended to use the same tactics for Ireland–Holland as he had in the Ireland–Egypt game. When he insisted on asking the question Charlton got up to leave. When he was halfway across the room I told him that he could not decide which journalists he would answer questions from and which he would ignore. He told me that I was Dunphy's mate, I told him I was Dunphy's colleague, not wanting to tell him that I was, in fact, his bodyguard.

Charlton looked at me for a moment. His stare was fierce and concentrated. He seemed to me, in that brief eyeball-to-eyeball encounter, a pretty formidable fellow. He walked out of the room.

The Italian journalists were amazed; the Irish journalists now had a story: Dunphy and Charlton in grand confrontation. It made headlines in both of Dublin's evening papers. On the way out of the press centre, Charlton called Dunphy 'a bitter little man'.

The following day the Ireland–Holland match was to take place. By now all the fans knew about Dunphy's outburst on television and his row with Charlton at the press conference. In his novel *The Van*, which is set in a Dublin ablaze with excitement during the 1990 World Cup, Roddy Doyle has his characters use the word Dunphy to mean 'sausage' since both resemble the male sexual organ.

Doyle made this up, but it captures the anti-Dunphy feeling alive in Dublin that summer.

We took a bus from the hotel to the ground. There were Irish supporters everywhere. They were in groups and most of them were bigger than myself and Dunphy put together. I wondered if there was another way of getting into the stadium without having to meet all these fans. I searched in vain for Italian police. But Dunphy said it was fine, if we walked towards the stadium in a normal way no one would touch him. He was right: a few supporters came up and asked him if he had any spare tickets. He shook his head and shrugged. In the background, a few groups of supporters shouted abuse. At the beginning of the match they chanted: 'If you hate Eamon Dunphy, clap your hands', but as it went on they began singing 'Come on you boys in green' and 'Ooo, aah, Paul McGrath'.

After the match the Press waited to see if Dunphy would force another confrontation. But Dunphy kept away: he wanted to make a serious point about the way Irish TV soccer was being played.

He went back to Ireland, which was now in an even greater excitement and fever over football. As the controversy raged about his comments on the team, Irish television showed the clip of him throwing his pen down and saying that whoever sent the team out to play in that manner ought to be ashamed of themselves. But fans were sure that he had said he was ashamed to be Irish, and swore Irish TV had doctored the tape.

He came to Italy once more for the final match and flew home just before the team. The road from the airport to the city was lined with fans and the city centre was packed with people ready to welcome the team home. The plane with the players on board circled the city to show them the welcome which was being prepared for them. Had they looked carefully at a point just beyond the airport they could have seen a group trying to turn over Eamon Dunphy's car as he tried to drive into the city. It was ugly, and for a few moments it could have gone either way, but in the end Dunphy managed to get home safely.

He had work to do now on his biography of Sir Matt Busby. He kept his head down. Soon, it was felt, the fans would forget about him. But if he thought life was going to be peaceful from now on, he was wrong. Irish radio had for some years run a satirical programme on Saturday mornings which no one listened to. But the winter after the World Cup a new series began called *Scrap Saturday* and slowly it picked up a mass audience.

Dermot Morgan, the main satirist, was superb at imitating Dunphy's voice, his mannerisms and phrasing. 'It was a good game, but not a great game,' the Dunphy persona kept saying until this became boring. *Scrap Saturday* needed to change and one Saturday morning they made Dunphy pregnant with John Giles as the father and week after week we were treated to news of the pregnancy. One Saturday, almost the complete show was devoted to the delivery, with the Dunphy character squealing with pain, wondering if it was a good delivery or a great delivery.

Dunphy didn't need a bodyguard any more. When he stopped his car at traffic lights, or went out to the shop to get cigarettes, people no longer shouted abuse, they asked him how the baby was. Sometimes he laughed about it. He continued working on his book, getting up to write at five o'clock every morning. It is what happens, he understood, when you speak your mind in a small country which has invented a new set of heroes. He would do it again, he says, and the more he has since found out about the Irish team and the World Cup, the more he knows he was right. There's a passage in Frank Stapleton's autobiography which he particularly relishes: 'Jack (Charlton) likes to think that he has got the Press where he wants them, but in the case of Eamon Dunphy he cannot get anywhere.'

1992

Becker

GORDON BURN

'Hit hard, play loud, leave a trail of broken strings,' it says across the sweat-slicked back of the young American player, Luke Jensen. He slips off the practice court straight into the clutches of the little Riviera tennis buds, flaunting their jeans *l'authentique blue* and *le vrai black*, their funkoid *chaussures de basket* and *nouveaux Ray-Ban circulaires*, while their mothers and grandmothers work their Chanel and petition for the best (Rainier-rubbing) positioning on the lunchtime *terrasse* at the Monte Carlo Country Club (MCCC). 'La saison est lancée, et fort bien,' as it will be announced in the following morning's *Nice-Matin*.

The slogan Jensen is wearing is a cheeky reworking of Mark McCormack's perennial exhortation to the suits of the super-corporate International Marketing Group: 'Work hard, work long, work smart.'

Although he earned something in the region of $200,000 in prize money in 1991, Jensen is part of the post-Agassi, fuck-Persil, anti-jock school of grime and grunge. The look is Mickey Rourke as the LA poet Charles Bukowski in *Barfly*, and the skid-row tailoring – the whacked-out T-shirt is matched with shineyed-up chopped-off denims – sits well with the lank hair, the goatee beard, the bitten nails, the bar-bum pallor, the lively gleam in the barely open eyes.

Jensen's face is difficult to read, set as it is against a strip of flashing sea and a bleached-out sky across which hang-gliders drift blithely as they ride the thermals of the high Corniche. His face is blurred away at the edges and smeared looking, the way it would be if you glimpsed it through smoky glass.

But enough remains to see that Jensen, ranked in the low-hundreds on the ATP computer, is still on the up-curve of achievement, hungry for scalps: there are no signs yet of satiety or self-disgust; no hints of jet-droop, fan-fatigue, of the scooped-out jaded look of realized ambition. This by itself is enough to distinguish him from the player practising on a back court whom the crowd is now surging past Jensen in a feeding frenzy to see.

Pat Cash once said that the courts at Monte Carlo made him feel more than usually like a performing animal. 'They're, like, sunk down so people walk along the top, and it's surrounded by a fence and there's two tennis players in there, and the people sort of stroll around and look at you. You feel like a zoo.'

In Boris Becker's case, better make that a monkey mena-gerie. Becker is out having a hit with his Davis Cup team-mate, Michael Stich, the player who demolished him in three sets in last year's Wimbledon final. That match was remark-able for the anguished wailing coming from Becker and for the vituperative verbal punishment he directed at himself; between games he screamed into his towel and even tried to take bites out of it; occasionally between points he smashed himself about the head with his racket or beat his head against the backstop canvas.

It was a performance I'd seen repeated eight days earlier in Barcelona, as Becker found himself going out in the first round to a young Spanish player languishing 200 or 300 places below him on the computer. The match had gone on court 24 hours late because of rain, and this was a problem. Then, as he threw the ball up to serve, Becker found that a 'Winston' advertising blimp was in his sightline.

Signboards all over the court, of course, as well as everybody on it, were imprinted with either the Winston name or that of Renault, Perrier, IBM or Reebok, Winston's cosponsors. Two bims in red Winston livery would flank Becker at the post-match press conference, a further reminder of the ongoing, global, mega-dollar transaction in which he is a star participant. But pursuing their corporate objectives in the air-space where he was struggling to stay in a tennis match was an ad opportunity too many. Becker ditched his racket and kicked the balls away in exasperation.

He has complained loudly over the years about the market-obsessed environment in which he has to play, and about having to be logoed to the eyeballs every time he sets foot in a public place. He has talked of having 'no inner calm, no peace'; about being 'a product, a puppet on a string, a marionette'.

His public statements have echoed John McEnroe's recently expressed opinion that: 'They are trying to turn us into money whores. It's obscene.' Becker's personal worth has been put at around $30 million, but it could be greater by a factor of as much as five if he didn't give the finger to most of the commercial opportunities that come his way. 'They say "a million". And then you say "No",' he has said. 'And then they offer – because they think everybody has his price – three million. And then you say "No" again. It feels good to know that I don't come cheap.'

He has contributed to Greenpeace and frequently donates money to charity. He has spoken up for squatters and the unemployed and helped Ion Tiriac, his manager, build an orphans' village in Romania which will be completed by the end of the year.

'I know him very well because he was living in my home many, many times,' says Nikki Pilic, the German Davis Cup captain. 'And Boris is one interesting person. He is all contradiction. He is *all* contradiction. For me he is like the painter Van Gogh. He's not . . . *usual*. He is making a lot of moves in the very last moment, and always the right moves. He didn't live at *all* normal life, and now he is thinking recently he wants to live a normal life.'

'I always tried to live like a normal guy growing up,' McEnroe told *Tennis* magazine earlier this year. 'I think that urge for normalcy, together with getting married and having kids, helped save me from becoming a burned-out, completely bitter cynic by 30. That's why I feel for Boris. One second he can't be better, the next he can't be worse. I can see it – it's like looking in a mirror.'

Boris-watchers are constantly on the look-out for the outward signs of fresh stress-cracks in his psyche. The towel chewing and big-match head banging are easy. Then there's the refusal of eye contact, the rapid blinking, the stammer . . .

The last three were all in evidence when Becker was eventually persuaded to take questions in the press tent in Barcelona. Unlike Borg who, in his twilight years, has learned to trot out blandnesses and well-lubricated generalizations, Becker, desperate to be 'real', still labours under the misapprehension that he is expected to engage with his questioner and actually *say something* in these rituals of mutual humiliation.

He sat under the Winston banner, between the Winston bims, behind a sign that said 'IBM' and gave the appearance of being somebody not only hemmed in by a business process against which he feels powerless, but of a man stigmatized by the burry logos he is obliged to wear on his chest, arms, thigh and ankle: half-bulletin board, half-person. The scruffiness – ratty hair, smudged forehead, a scurvy three-day growth – was perhaps in reaction to this. What was he? A survivor of the McDonald's gunman, motorway carnage, the mad axe man, the towering inferno? A blind diagnosis would be post-traumatic stress disorder. How does it *feel*? Sometimes he stared out with what looked like hate in his eyes. Afterwards, on the short walk back to the players' lounge, few felt brave enough to intrude on his particular private grief.

'He's in a foul mood,' Richard Evans reported back. 'He doesn't want to talk the way he's feeling because he thinks he'll probably say something he'll regret.' Evans's card says 'Vice-President, Communications, the Association of Tennis Professionals' and he is one of the few channels of communication Becker has left open to the world.

'Some days he can be very chatty,' Evans says. 'Other days I can walk into the locker-room and he looks like he's never seen me before in his life.' Becker's current coach, Tomas Smid, is forbidden by the terms of his contract from talking to the press. Gunther Bosch, who discovered Becker as an eight-year-old and brought him to the attention of Ion Tiriac eight years later, became an unperson when he put his name to a picture-book of Boris at work and play.

And still the lady from *Hola!* ('I can't go in the restaurant in these old ski clothes,' she said of an outfit that could have done service at Stringfellows) was at a loss to know why Boris refused to throw open the doors of his love nest to her, unlike that sweet Stefan Edberg whose wedding she was covering in Sweden the following week. 'Do you think the new Boris girlfriend is attractive?' she wanted to know. '*Do* you? The black one? I don't think she is good-looking at all.'

Becker once talked about the 'eroticism' he sensed between himself and the people who come to watch him play. 'I know they are silently looking me up and down. I always react in the same embarrassed way. I bend down and tie my shoes although it's unnecessary. They don't only want to see you — they want to have you.'

The gallery crowding round to watch Becker practising with Michael Stich at Monte Carlo is a shifting one: once they have fixed him on their Nikomatics and Akais and Supazooms (the auto-focuses noiselessly shifting and stirring in an oddly sensual way) they get bored watching his power serves and singing topspun back hands and athleticism around the court and wander on.

The girl with the bare midriff, though, has established herself in a prime position at the end of the baseline, just above where Becker is serving, and she's giving way to nobody. She is shaking with the effort of maintaining her posture (no unsightly folding flesh). But she is also shaking with something else. Behind the shield of her dark glasses, her eyes never stray from Becker.

'Bello! . . . Bello!' the middle-aged Italian woman standing next to me croons repeatedly. 'Oh! . . . Boom-boom!'

Unlike Stich, who appears loose, unselfconscious, Becker has the by now familiar look of somebody who feels they are, as he has admitted, 'game to be hunted'; somebody who is finding life 'a lot of hard work for very little fun'.

'Look, my friend,' the manager Tiriac says. 'If you don't want to be there and looked at in the arena, go in the factory where nobody is going to look at you. *Ever.* Make your fuckin' $2,000 a month and shut your goddam big fuckin' mouth. You know, I'm sure that if Boris would go right now to Moscow and work three years in a homeless organization there, he's going to appreciate differently the value of the life when he comes out. You cannot take only the good things and wipe out the other things.'

Tiriac first caught Becker in action on the same court where he has just been practising, in Monte Carlo in 1984. Ille Nastase was yesterday's papers; Guillermo Vilas's playing days were coming to an end, and Tiriac was sniffing round for hot young blood.

'The guy couldn't run, the guy couldn't do anything,' he says now of the fifteen-year-old Boris Becker. 'It was the worst athlete I ever saw in my life. But he was bleeding on the knees, he was bleeding on his mouth, he was diving all over, he wanted very badly. I mean, I can make an athlete. I don't have a problem. Give him bloody six months on the stairs, three hours a day, comes an athlete and plays like a machine. No problem. I can make him hit a tennis ball from any*where*.

'So. He wanted very badly. He had this will-power; the desire. And I say, okay, I will take another one, then thank you very much, good-bye. Looked like a very determined kid.'

The hospitality tent where we are sitting, complete with sun divans and a butler butling and a large sign bearing Tiriac's name, is evidence of the progress he has made in the world. He grew up in Romania – 'I started from very, very low, and very hard. I made my way up with my shoulders and my hands' – and has little patience with Becker's carpings about the privations of the celebrity life.

'I know that Boris is just a normal teenager,' he says, 'although he's 25 now. I look at him going through *stages*. And he went through a very idealistic stage.'

This is thought to have had its beginnings in a visit Becker made to his former girlfriend Karen Schultz's family in East Germany in the last days of the Cold War. He has recently come out against a reunified Germany staging the Olympic Games in the year 2000, and condemned the growing support for neo-Nazi groups in Europe. 'Stop this hatred, shocked Becker begs Nazi racists,' ran the headlines earlier this year over reports that his girlfriend, Barbara Feltus, a black woman, was facing an 'unbelievable' daily barrage of abuse, 'which has left her feeling terrified'.

'I now experience nationalism,' Becker said. 'So much

attention is on my skin and the colour of my girlfriend's skin. It shows me how many extreme right-wing people there are now in Germany.'

'I think Boris is very brave to say all these things,' Nikki Pilic says. 'I think if he lives in a democracy, and Boris Becker is a big product of that democracy, he should express his opinion. I don't have the feeling he goes with a black girlfriend just because he wants to provoke somebody.'

Tiriac would second this. He draws the line, however, at Boris's championing of squatters' rights. 'I think there was *nothing* in it. But what this shows is that Boris is a human being who is much more interested in other things than in a tennis ball.' Pause. 'Very important, though. *Fuckin'* important, tennis balls. If you hit one less, you go, and nobody is talking to you any more.'

I asked him how frustrating it is for him to have Becker giving the thumbs down to virtually all the deals he puts together.

'He doesn't make ten per cent of his money on the court. [Becker won $1,228,708 in 1991.] He can double that, or triple that. I could make him $2 million tomorrow morning. More.

'So to deal with Boris is not easy. But it is his life. I am very philosophical about this thing. It doesn't matter. The money I make with Boris is almost . . . idealistic. I put forward on the table whatever I think he should take. After that it's his privilege. It is very easy to say no when you make ten times over what you need.

'But to return to your *frustrating* for a moment. I am frustrated because he didn't win another ten Grand Slams by now. I think this guy could have won three times more. Five times more. He has the possibility. Now the question in life is would he have been happier? *I* don't know. He's a very emotional young man. He looks on the outside completely different than he is inside. He's a very mild, sensitive human being, Boris. He's still at 25 trying to find himself. He's trying to *find* himself.'

And his increasingly erratic behaviour on court and off these days?

'I take it to mean he is a human. I take it to mean that he is going along the same route that they all go along. They cannot cope. They cannot difference the good and the bad; they cannot difference the right and the wrong; they cannot difference the white and the black; they cannot difference when to say no and when to say yes. They're going step by step every day in another life – another level. Then it is very important who you have around. Jeezus. It's much more important almost than your original parents at that stage. Your surroundings, they make you or break you.

'But I can tell you this, my friend. I prefer a Boris to somebody who goes there every day with the same face, comes out with the same face, is going to die with the same face, and doesn't *live*. This guy lives. It's *life* in him. For good or for bad. Boris is a guy that is a fair guy once you get to his heart.'

'Youthful success especially can mean that one becomes symbolic before one is real,' Leo Braudy writes in *The Frenzy of Renown*. 'Created by others before one can create oneself . . . in the course of the 20th century, the public's ability to create instant fame and thereby satisfy its own sense of fulfilment becomes more powerful, even as the stresses on those so plucked out and ennobled become more severe.'

Becker operates within a forcefield that only his girlfriend, it seems, and Tiriac can safely enter. At home in Monaco, he doesn't answer the phone before ten a.m. and after that it is likely you will have to communicate with him through Barbara Feltus. This applies even to Tiriac.

At Barcelona he didn't want to talk to me because he had a match coming up, and then he didn't want to talk because he was beaten. A meeting in Monte Carlo was set up for the following week and then, 24 hours before it was due to happen, cancelled.

Over three days, the time was never judged right to tell Becker that I was hanging around hoping to see him. Tiriac said he would intervene, but then Boris was never available. Kicking my heels in a Monaco bar one midnight I watched Tiriac stroll in with a woman companion. This, it transpired, was the former Monaco police chief's daughter, Benedicte Courtin, whom Tiriac expelled from Wimbledon in 1987, claiming she was 'distracting' Becker from the defence of his title. Tiriac said he would call Boris 'first thing' in the morning. He called first thing, got Barbara Feltus, and I was on the next flight home.

There are two ways of getting to Nice airport from Monaco: by road, along the Côte d'Azur or by helicopter. Within seconds the helicopter is over water, dragging its shadow across the swimming pools and sherbety villas of Monte Carlo, Ville Franche, Cap Ferrat and other places that live, as the brochures have it, where luxury lives; spinning up and out of Boris Becker's life – sphere, star, speck, to quote Updike – like the sweetest-struck ball.

Somewhere down there, Boris still wasn't answering his phone.

1992

The Agony of Being a Fan

NICK HORNBY

August 1991, and Arsenal, my team, the reigning champions, take the field against QPR for the first game of the new season. They receive a rapturous reception, which is as it should be: here, after all, are the players who have lost just one league game in the previous fifteen months, the players who are widely expected to terrify the rest of the continent in the European Cup, the team with the best strike force and the meanest defence in the First Division. Our love for them is boundless, our optimism inexhaustible. They start the game slowly, and noisy devotion becomes baffled silence. When Dennis Bailey puts Rangers one up, the Bloke Behind Me can take it no more. 'You're *rubbish*, Arsenal,' he bawls. 'Dixon, you're a *wanker*.'

In less than half an hour, the rapture has vanished into the ether and Highbury is once more what I have always known it to be – a refuge for depressives and malcontents, whingers and whiners. We are getting what we paid for and all is right with the world.

My first bout of football pain came on March 15, 1969, when on my first visit to Wembley I watched Swindon Town of the Third Division destroy Arsenal with two goals in extra time. I was eleven years old, and I honestly believe that I was too young to cope, that my father should never have taken me to the game, that if he had been a responsible parent he would have recognized the potential for trauma that the afternoon contained. He compounded this appalling error of judgment by standing up to applaud the winners, a misguided attempt at gallantry which resulted in me trying to run out of the stadium and refusing to talk to him all the way home.

I was the only Arsenal supporter in my entire year at school. In the Sixties – with Charlton, Law and Best at United, Greaves at Spurs, Marsh at Rangers, Moore, Hurst and Peters at West Ham – you had to be some kind of deranged flagellant to choose a team that hadn't won a thing since the Coronation. It was wholly predictable, then, that at about 8.50 on the morning of Monday, March 17, I was lying face down in the grammar school dirt with 30 jeering first formers on my back. It would not be whimsical to suggest that I still go to Arsenal now because of what Swindon did to me then: like a gambler who keeps playing because it is the only way to win back what he has lost, I still feel, somewhere in me, that I am owed for what Ian Ure and Jon Sammels and Bobby Gould put me through that afternoon.

Since then, of course, I have lost big several more times. York City, Tranmere, Wrexham . . . And Wembley itself has become a giant Room 101. Sometimes, just as I am drifting off to sleep, I can see Don Rogers running the length of the pitch to slip the ball past Bob Wilson, or Allan Clarke's diving header past Geoff Barnett in 1972, or Willie Young presenting Ipswich Town's Roger Osborne with an unmissable chance in 1978, or Nigel Winterburn's penalty miss ten years later or Seaman palming Lineker's cross-shot into the corner of the net in last year's semi-final.

I don't recall the good times I've had at Wembley with anything like the same frequency – not just because there haven't been as many of them (my personal Wembley record is played ten, won two, lost *eight*), but because when you support a football team, misery is the only currency that can purchase real ecstasy. And if pain is wealth, then all of us, apart from Liverpool fans, are as rich as Croesus.

Arsenal supporters have been luckier than most of late: we have at least had something to spend it on. Two Championships in four seasons, and a Littlewoods Cup win over Liverpool the year before that ... There are countless fans who would feel I am singularly unqualified to write about pain and football. How does it feel to follow, say, Luton Town? How much does *that* hurt?

The most committed football fan I have ever met, Neil Kaas, watches his team home and away, but this he regards as just a tiny part of the job, like opening the mail. The rest of the time he worries, and argues, and sulks, and attends Luton Town open evenings (although his ferocity is such that he is no longer very welcome at these). Currently, he is harassing Luton Council for a statue to commemorate Raddy Antic, whose last-minute goal at Maine Road, a decade or so back, prevented Luton from dropping into Division Two. Neil Kaas has lived with football agony for most of his life.

Despite relegation on the last day of the season (which he regards as something of a relief, peace at last for a terminally ill football team), his favourite, most lovingly cherished day of suffering remains April 13, 1985. Luton were 1–0 up against Everton in an FA Cup semi-final; Sheedy equalized with four minutes left, and Mountfield scored the winner in extra time. He is still bitter. 'All Friday night they'd been showing Sheedy free kicks on the box. The only one who wasn't watching was our goalkeeper.'

This was the closest Neil had ever come to Wembley and on the way home that night he came to the conclusion that this was the closest he would ever come in his entire life. 'People say you get over it, but you don't, not really, not properly.' On Sunday 14, he spent the day in the dark, with the curtains drawn, until his mother complained. A request to light a memorial candle – his family is Jewish – was met with a blank and insensitive refusal. He couldn't read a newspaper for a week ('Too many pictures'). Even the Live Aid concert that July distressed him – 'I should never have gone. I kept looking up at the Royal Box and thinking, "Stevie Foster would have stood there."'

He is aware, as we are all aware, that the sudden-death coronary shocks of the FA Cup offer only one kind of pain. Neil is wounded every year by his team's refusal even to score at Old Trafford (they managed a goal up there 21 years ago, but he makes the long trek every season anyway), and by the permanent car boot sale that Luton indulge in. 'If a player makes a promising debut on the Saturday, I'm frightened to turn on Teletext on Monday, in case they've flogged him.' There is the pain of watching arch-rivals succeed where you have failed dismally (the only Cup Final Neil has never watched involved Watford). And for supporters of more ambitious clubs, there is the long, slow death of Championship dreams, where hope is extinguished little by little, week by week, until one cold wet January afternoon, you're 1–0 down at home to Southampton, and you write the rest of the year off and start looking forward to August again.

There are those who would argue that this discomfort is not real, that sport cannot matter enough to break anyone's heart, but this is simply not the case. For some of us, the desire to see our team win at Wembley, or become league champions, or gain promotion from Division Three, is the only *consistent* ambition we have ever held. Whatever we want from our lives now – the Booker Prize, a recording contract, a promotion, a Porsche convertible, the girl at the Virgin Megastore checkout desk – we cannot possibly have coveted it for as long as we have cherished dreams of football glory, dreams which have remained fundamentally unchanged since childhood.

Imagine that you have been studying for 20 years for a qualification that will change your life, or waiting the same length of time to hear about a job you have applied for, the only job you have ever really wanted. Now imagine receiving the news that you have been unsuccessful ... *and everyone around you standing and cheering wildly*. If you can grasp the dizzying, nauseating, stinging injustice and humiliation of such a moment, then you can grasp how Neil Kaas felt when Sheedy bent his free kick round the Luton wall and into the top corner. The fact that the game itself is trivial, and, of course, in most ways it is, does not mean that it cannot inflict real pain.

In May 1989, after a home league defeat by Derby that seemed to have cost Arsenal the chance of their first Championship since 1971, I felt as low as it is possible to feel after a football match. That evening, I went to see *King Lear* at the Old Vic, but I was unable to shake off my self-pity and I couldn't for the life of me see what the old git was moaning about. At least he'd *been* king – he hadn't blown it the week before the Coronation, like we had. I vowed then, as I have vowed many times before and since, that I would never again make myself so vulnerable to the team, that I would get them off my back and out of my life if it was the last thing I did.

Two weeks later, however, Michael Thomas scored his stunning last-minute Championship-winning goal at Anfield to provide me and thousands like me with the most intense moment of our lives. The timing of the goal was a vital ingredient of this delirium, of course (I for one had given up all hope by then), as was the venue (we hadn't won up there for decades); but what really gave the night meaning was the anxiety and despair, year after year after year of it, that had gone before. I spent every last penny of my hoarded misery that night, blew eighteen years' worth on one split second, and it felt better than anyone who is not a fan can ever be expected to understand. When Arsenal won the league again two years later, it didn't feel the same – partly because it was achieved in a less dramatic fashion, but mostly because I had nothing left.

So being a fan is mostly about replenishment, and last year provided me with plenty of that; outplayed by Benfica, two or three months of dismal ineptitude in the league around Christmas, and then the Wrexham humiliation . . . I began to feel whole again. The genius of the football supporter is that he has managed to convert something as unappetizing and unpromising as an English football season into something from which he can take pleasure. Manchester United fail to win the Championship for 25 years in a row, but attract the biggest crowds of all; Everton supporters turn up in their thousands week after week, ignoring the better, winning team that plays a matter of yards away; the absence of Gascoigne and Lineker will not deter the Tottenham faithful.

Meanwhile, Neil Kaas will be watching his team lose to Brentford and Peterborough, red-faced with rage and frustration, and I'll be there when we go out of the Cup at home to Middlesbrough, say, or Manchester City. The quality of football will be poor (we know that already, most of us), the weather foul, the environment uncomfortable at best, intimidating at worst. There will be sweet moments for all of us, but they will be swamped by the sour . . . and we'll all be happy, in our own peculiar way, saving up for a sunny day two or three years off in the future.

1992

In Search of the Silver King

JAMES FOX

One morning, at around six, the telephone rings in my room in a motel in Islamorada. It's late May and a gale is getting up outside, the warm wind streaming through the palms, the white lines of the tennis courts below still obscured in darkness. 'It's unspeakable,' says the voice of Robert Hughes from a few doors down the balcony. 'It's a bloody wind tunnel,' he says. 'We'll fish live bait.' And he slams down the phone.

The monotone voice of the TV weather channel has been crackling in my half sleep, recycled every fifteen minutes over still ads of the local marine suppliers. What I'm hearing is heartbreaking. We have three days to fish for the tarpon, and the report – a low pressure front south of Cuba, an opposing system down from Maine – predicts wind and rain. This will be put into perspective by my guide, Captain Bud Grace, as the worst weather for this season for 35 years, which is exactly as long as he's been fishing the flats, the 'backcountry' as they call it in this revered little fishopolis, 100 miles down from Miami.

Live bait is nothing like casting with a fly. It's like taking four shots for the green, instead of shooting a hole in one. Tarpon are the mightiest and most exciting and, for their jumping, the most spectacular fish you can catch on light

tackle (perhaps on any tackle). You fish them inshore in
shallow water, just you and a guide in a small boat. Casting
at them with a fly, at 60 or 70 feet, as they ghost across the
sandy flats in the green and white water, is the skilful,
exhilarating way to fish them; a mixture of fishing and
stalking, requiring delicate skills with the line and rod, requiring, theoretically, perfect casting.

You rarely see the salmon or trout that you cast for, but
with the tarpon you cast a few feet ahead of its dark form as
it suddenly appears out of the shadows and channels. Then if
you're lucky, you feel its tremendous power. BOOM is the
word always used, the tarpon-speak of the marina bars, the
fist smacking upward into the palm to describe the fierce
take. Then, whatever your skill, the question is: will your
heart stand up to it, to the next few minutes as it flies and
plunges, before the muscles settle in for anything from 40
minutes to five hours of struggle with a fish that weighs
around 100 or 150lb (the record on a fly is 187lb). You have
the same fight with live bait, of course, but it's not much to
do with skill whether the tarpon takes your wriggling mullet,
suspended from a cork float and flung out from the skiff.

Hughes is a chronically early riser, whose prodigious writing
output is usually over by 11 a.m., and the combat-ready
hours of the Islamorada regime suit him perfectly happily. He
has already been shopping for breakfast at 5 a.m., striding to
the general store across a darkened Highway One in a T-shirt
that says 'Andrea Mantegna', laying out his recent top-of-the-
line purchases on the motel floor: a twelve-weight, nine-foot
Sage rod; Marine Phospherbronze reels in little suede bags;
Scientific Anglers Tarpon Taper line, forward weighted and
floating; a box of outrageously vulgar flies, of feather and
mirror strips of mylar, with little simulated fish eyes made of
links from a lamp chain. 'Deranged drag queens' is what they

look like to him, and since nobody knows why the tarpon takes the fly, they are clearly designed only with other tarpon fly-tiers in mind. All this gear is useless for live bait.

Hughes has also had time – before calling me – to read a chunk of *Double Whammy*, the latest novel by Carl Hiaasen, the reporter from the *Miami Herald* who often writes about corruption in fishing tournaments in Florida. Double Whammy is the name of a lure, used locally. There is also 'Beulah's Bush' (black and purple), 'Stendhal' (red and black – the literary fly), 'Hothead' and 'Black Death'.

'How's yer casting?' he had asked on the phone from New York, as a form of invitation to this trip. 'Can yer double haul? *Double haul*.' Evidently not. 'You'll have 30 feet of line lying in the boat and you'll have to get it out pretty quick,' he said. 'When it takes, you'll have something on with the power of an MG, and the eccentric flying habits of a Tiger Moth. It's got jaws like cinder blocks. It's like a giant herring, with enormous scales, this intense silver . . .' He tells me in detail about double hauling, but I'm not concentrating. I'm on my way to Florida. 'See you there, mate.'

I knew about this fish because it had helped to break up my grandmother's first marriage in 1912. Her millionaire husband, fresh from Harvard and the Porcellian club, followed only the sporting calendar, usually in a haze of alcohol: Aiken for hunting, Georgia for quails and down to Florida for 'Mr Tarpon', as he called it in his affectionate, but doomed letters. In those days it was a trip into the wilderness. Finally, she could take no more. And wasn't Lord Cowdray, fishing for tarpon in 1910 in Tampico, stranded there for two years when the Mexican revolution broke out?

The obsession and reverence, the *love* that surrounds the tarpon, which is greater than any I have come across, has much to do with its strange prehistoric beauty, its Leviathan looks – the ancient toothless jaw that closes upwards like the ramp of a landing craft, and opens in a Jonah-swallowing square scoop; its large, leopard-like eyes (perhaps the origin of its name Megalops Atlanticus), whose iris is the colour of old oxidized gold. And the black, black pupil. The thick pearly scales on its back are the size and shape of artichoke leaves and its sides and belly are that intense silver, dazzling in the sun as it leaps, and particularly startling when you fish at night with lights.

Instead of teeth it has a sandpapered mouth. Its gills, which rattle when it leaps, are like flattened plates of dulled steel, so sharp they will slice a 125lb test leader effortlessly if it gets snagged. The sound of a tarpon taking a fly on the surface is a loud pneumatic crack, plus a suction and snap that reminds you of what life is like down there where there are no manners.

The tarpon has *character*, smartness. It's a little spooked, perhaps, by the memory of its bird predators when it was a fry, or by its own predator, the hammerhead shark. And it's no good to eat. You fish them to the boat, cut tackle and release them, by law. The hooks will rust away.

Islamorada is the best place for tarpon up and down this coast – and one of the best in the world – because of the number and variety of its sandflats. And this is the best time. In the colder months the fish lie off in deeper water south of Key West or in the Gulf of Mexico, feeding on crab and squid. Then in early March they start their northward migration, spawning in the shallow water of the Keys. Islamorada is only four miles from the Gulf Stream, its edge marked by the Alligator light – so that offshore boats put out from here too. The tarpon don't like all this activity – particularly the jetskiers – and are making themselves scarcer as the years go by. 'How would you like a Ferrari driving through your living room four times a day?' said one of my guides, indignantly.

★

On the morning of day one, this day of wind, we are due for check-in at 7 a.m. at Bud 'n Mary's Marina, 'The Sportfishing Capital of the World', a mile down the road, where our guides are waiting with their skiffs. The first day of term. Who will be the captains, the bullies, the comedians? How soon will I be found out?

A serious cook, although sometimes compulsive with the ingredients, Hughes prepares our breakfast in his self-catering suite along the balcony. It looks as if it might be *œufs sur le plat* (fried eggs) *au bacon*. The motel room is rattling with adrenalin. As I search his bathroom for shaving cream, which I have left behind, Hughes says, sharply: 'You won't find any shaving cream, mate, because I haven't got any.' I detect that this is typical of what whingeing pommies bring as extra baggage. The Australian has applied water and steel to the fearlessly articulate jaw just like Crocodile Dundee with his hunting knife.

We have fished together before, racing across the glassy water from Shelter Island to Plum Gut and Block Island Sound on early summer mornings for bluefish, to join the other punters in a haze of gasoline and a bleeping of Hummingbird fish finders. There one morning, my young son discovered what a simile was, when we struck into a plentiful shoal of fish and Hughes exclaimed, reeling up maniacally, 'Christ, it's like rats in a bloody basement.' But hauling up fighting bluefish requires almost no skill at all.

At the exact hour, with nervous precision, we draw into Bud 'n Mary's, a movie-set marina with Hollywood-size billboard lettering and a fibreglass great white shark creaking in the wind. A tame egret of blinding whiteness and ceramic delicacy is pacing the top of the bait tank picking bits of shrimp. A beautiful young woman, dressed in dirty overalls, is ladling out live mullet from her truck into plastic buckets for the guides – a Jessica Lange among a couple of dozen would-be Sam Shepards.

The skiffs, eighteen of them, are suspended on electric winches in their covered stalls along the dock, like a stable of polo ponies – stripped-down craft with 150 horsepower engines and little else except radio. The names of their jockeys are posted up, including my three guides: Captain 'Joe' Johannsen, Captain Jack Backus and Captain Bud Grace. In the office I purchase Polaroids, without which you cannot see the tarpon underwater. Everyone down here knows Robert Hughes, of course – he's one of the most popular skiff designers in Miami. Hughes has said he's from *Time* magazine, but he's left out that he's its art critic. A guide says, 'Hey how's it going?' A woman replies: 'Better than the average bimbo, I guess.'

In the centre of the yard is a wooden sign that reads 'This is Why'. It is a dated homily from the days of muscular Christianity and Teddy Roosevelt: 'Far better it is to dare mighty things, to win glorious triumphs even though checkered with failure than to take ranks with those poor spirits who neither enjoy much nor suffer much because they live in the grey twilight that knows not victory or defeat.' Hughes gets into his skiff, sits like a Buddha as they push off and says with equal muscularity in front of the guides: 'If you catch a fish and I don't, I'll fucking kill you.'

The thrill of these early mornings is the racing at high speed in the damp salty wind towards the fishing grounds. You see the beauty of the soft changing light on the sandbars, the stands of palms on the distant keys, the lines of marking posts curving into the ocean as in the Venetian lagoon. The highway, always visible, becomes tiny, the miniature trucks slipping silently back and forth across the elegant arch of the causeway.

Captain 'Joe' Johannsen, a thick-set man in his fifties with Bogart mannerisms, is not interested in bait, and insists on fly, despite the high wind. Nor is he much interested in my shaky credentials as a salmon fisherman. He says, simply, 'I prefer salt-water fish. They hit harder. You can get more out of them.' When I say I may need practice, he says: 'Well, how good is your casting?' He soon finds out.

We haul up on the Gulf side of the highway, the flexible fibreglass pole dug in and bending as it holds the boat against the wind. At first it's a disaster. Unused to the fierce power of this rod and the heavy line, I cast all over the place, tensing up, slapping the water, whipping the monofilament, casting short. In the high wind a back cast swerves and the hook hammers into my back, and sticks in my shirt. I can feel the point on my skin. 'You better watch that,' says Captain Joe. 'These flies are exceedingly sharp.'

By 9 a.m. my arm is aching. I think I've forgotten how to cast. Then the truth, put politely: 'There's something you're doing wrong, Jim.' (There is no such name as James in America.) He reminds me: cast economically. Take the line from two inches above the water. Cast back to the stars; forward to the horizon. Let the rod do the work. And *calm down*. In a few minutes I'm casting simply and effectively, 50 feet, 60 feet, the line curling obediently on to the water.

We wait for six hours and see two fish. We talk about thriller writers. He's fished with a few of them – local boys. He is amused that they are famous. 'Ross Thomas. Writes fishing articles, right? You say he's *famous*?' The Bogart smile. He says, 'How do you start writing an article like this one you're doing?' I say the conventional way might be a moody lead about the weather, the pressure. Mention Cuba, if you like, but leave out Hemingway. No thees and thous. A few minutes later he turns around from staring for tarpon and says, 'Page one. It was blowing 25 to 30.' I say it's good, truthful. In the afternoon he says, 'Frankly, Jim, there's not a lot moving out here,' and we head home.

★

Day two dawns, with the wind still howling. Hughes and I both slept badly. He cooked a special dish for breakfast, *œufs au beurre noir*, the eggs edged with carbonized black lace, the yolks *baveuse*, the English muffins most heavily buttered.

All the guides have strangely different backgrounds. There are rumoured to be renegade coke smugglers in their band from the old days of the cigarette boats. Jack Backus, on the other hand, was a police officer in Seattle, a handsome guy, TJ Hooker type, 41, a fisherman from childhood. After six of his buddies were shot, he felt he 'wasn't meeting enough nice people'. He was getting tired, too, of putting on all that weaponry every morning to go to work – the 9mm pistol, the bulletproof vest, the steel shock-plate, the handcuffs, the knives and the shotguns. Then one day an armed suspect lowered his window and shot Backus's fellow patrolman in the face. 'So I was crouching beside the car shooting it out,' he said. 'And I'm talking about exchanging 200 rounds of ammunition. I was 20 years before retirement. And I said to myself, "I'm going bonefishing."'

We load up with mullet and pole up on the edge of a channel, windward of Indian Key – an island of barely ten acres which was once the Dade County seat but which has been uninhabited since the nineteenth century. The light changes rapidly on the water – powdery green, pale yellow, bleached white. At moments the sea is as defined as cultivated land: muddy plough, bright grass, dark fields of kale. It is a brisk morning by Florida standards. Leopard rays are leaping out of the spray, pelicans diving for fish. It is here that I get my first strike at a tarpon, around 8.15.

You quickly know the proximity of a tarpon with live bait – although barracuda can be mistaken for it – by the nervous wriggling of the mullet on the line, which you can feel in the rod, as the fish makes two or three passes at it. On the fourth pass the tarpon rolls over the bait and takes it and Backus yells, 'Strike!' and then screams, 'Reel, reel!' There are sudden jitters in the boat as if we're under attack. The tarpon, which Backus judges to be around 100lb, leaps and twists, just like a Tiger Moth, and then swims towards me, slacking the line.

I am so mesmerized by its appearance that I don't react fast enough — with the frenzied reflexes, the fierce attentiveness that you have to acquire for this — and lose the tension and the tarpon shakes free and is gone. Five minutes later, Backus strikes at another tarpon and hands me his rod while the fish is up in the air doing its silvery dance and I pull back instinctively to try and fix the hook instead of 'bowing' to him, pointing the rod at him and giving him line. His weight in the air snaps the leader and the tippett and he makes off.

Those few seconds with either fish — the electric power and strength I can feel through the rod against my muscles — is enough to secure my addiction. But the terrible grief, the sense of bereavement and loss, the *depression* I'm nursing would be comic if it weren't impossible to shake off. The worst for these guides is that fishermen talk about it endlessly in a jibberish of self-recrimination which would seem ridiculous to anyone else. It's only midday, and it's all we see. 'This is what I'll call our bad luck day, Jim,' says Backus.

Hughes has still not seen a single tarpon and we are moving through the familiar stages of most fishing expeditions. He recalls them for me: the optimism and excitement, followed by the lengthy anecdotage of failure, then the wounded camaraderie, the fear of showing your low spirits in case the other is still holding out, then the slim consolation of merely surviving the elements.

We will go to the canals, we will go to the bridges, fish at night. We could always go to Robbie's Marina down the road, where they swim around beside the dock, semi-tame, eating pinfish out of your hand. Robbie has been feeding them for 20 years and there are around 200 fish down there, many of them around 150lb. They would go for your lure without hesitation, but it's rumoured that Robbie has a night sight on his rifle. Shake your head slowly and say it: Robbie loves those fish.

For wisdom I visit Jimmy Allbright, senior angler and revered guide, now retired, who has fished here longer than anybody. He fished before the war with Hemingway, and more recently with Ted Williams, baseball's greatest ever and now, it is agreed, also the greatest fly fisherman in the land.

Allbright is tying flies, his forearms the deep colour of tobacco plugs and the texture of leather. His sitting room is adorned with tarponalia, the air filled with the screeching of macaws and parrots. He says he wouldn't even go out in this weather, because of the wind. He also says there are fewer and fewer tarpon about in the daytime now, that they are so 'run over' that they have abandoned the shallows, feeding at night and travelling in the Gulf Stream in deep water.

'I never used to hear of tarpon in the Gulf Stream and now you get shoals of 500 sighted by the offshore boats,' he said. Soon, he predicted, they'll be very scarce for fishermen – although the population is healthy – whereas in Hemingway's time, he seemed to suggest, the fish would leap into the boat and embrace the writer in its fins whenever he appeared.

Fossil remains of the tarpon date back 300 million years and suggest that they looked much the same then as they do now. The Seminole Indians of Florida incorporated their great age into one of their oldest myths. Before the arrival of man, as they have it, the Rocky Mountains formed the edge of the continent and were rich in silver mines. The Great Spirit commissioned the tarpon to guard them by swimming up and down in front of their underwater entrances, and re-warded them with silver-plated scales which he permitted them to renew every century by dipping themselves in a spring of liquid silver. As the land expanded, the fish were forced southwards to the Gulf of Mexico and beyond and lost their commission and white men eventually pillaged the unguarded mines. In gratitude, and out of pity, the Great Spirit decided to make the tarpon an eternal gift of their silver armour.

Will the Silver King – as they call it here – rise again on the third day? Or as God said to Job: 'Canst thou draw out Leviathan with an hook, or his tongue with a cord which thou lettest down?' Hughes is doing something artistic with the eggs, which I judge to be *œufs miroir* (fried eggs), accompanied by twists of bacon.

The wind has died a little and Captain Bud Grace, 35 years on the flats, ties a blue handkerchief under his eyes to ward off the skin cancer that has already scarred him and guns his skiff alongside the highway, just overtaking the yellow school bus, speeding expertly through narrow avenues of mangroves – slowing for the hidden mud banks. He knows every bay, cut, island and flat in these parts and his expertise is quickly obvious: he has chosen a place off Long Key, half an hour south off Islamorada, on the edge of a bright sandflat, 100 yards from a deep channel, surrounded by dark water so that the sandy area looks like a large stage on which the tarpon must appear.

There are three other boats within sight, all pitching in the wind, but somehow Captain Bud has chosen a spot on this open sea which is calm and sheltered by the surrounding shallowness. He's put on a new line, a bright yellow thirteen weight, forward biased and floating, and has blackened its end with magic marker to reduce the glare. He tries it out, with economical casts, his forearm hardly moving and says: 'Yeah, that shoots good. It might feel a little heavy, but it's good in the wind.'

Today, finally, I learn the mysteries of the double haul

from Bud Grace. 'A guy up at Islamorada went to this casting school for five days, cost him $500,' says Bud. 'Get a diploma and all that. He came out with this guide and started casting and the guide said, "You better go and get your money back."' He is in fits of laughter. '*Go and get your money back.*' he repeats. 'Now that was a low blow, wasn't it?'

On the back cast Bud pulls sharply on the line with his left hand, and again just before the forward cast. The line shoots forward at great speed, rattling through the guides. By putting a little extra speed on the line as you cast, it strains the rod and stores and releases a little more kinetic energy. The effect is remarkable, putting another ten feet on the cast, but it needs perfect timing.

There's a good reason to double haul. When the tarpon appears you have 30 feet of line on the floor of the casting deck, and you have to cast quickly. The double haul relieves you of making two or three false casts to get the line out. It saves time.

It was near here once that Bud Grace, with a client, had his longest haul with a tarpon, lasting seven hours and 20 minutes, until they lost it under the bridge. For much of that time a hammerhead shark was pursuing the tarpon, driven off by Bud gunning his motor, so that the hammerhead couldn't sense the vibrations of the fish on the line, and even running it off with the pole. 'We went for miles across the bay,' he said. 'When he (the client) went to the Green Turtle that night they had to lift the Martini to his lips.'

I'm getting used to spotting tarpon, but my eyes are not nearly as sharp as Bud's, who never takes his eyes off the water. A couple of hours pass. For breakfast he has a Granola bar, and soon after that a plug of Redman chewing tobacco. We talk about hurricanes. A monument in the centre of town commemorates 'The 35', as they call that hurricane here. Like all monuments to wars and disasters, it is necessarily misleading. A sandstone *bas-relief* shows the palm trees with their branches blown horizontally – but waving in art nouveau ripples like Ophelia's hair in the lilies. In fact, the wind stripped everything bare, leaving not a mangrove leaf the length of the keys.

It is inscribed to its victims, the residents 'and the war veterans' of Islamorada, the suggestion being that the *anciens combatants* had finally been killed in a glorious, separate struggle with the salt water, having failed to achieve glory on their first attempt in Flanders in 1915. Bud remembers Donna in 1960 which, he said, only claimed one life at Islamorada, given the satellite warning. Bud and his friends went 40 miles north, sat in a motel room and played poker all night. 'Next day all the bridges were out,' he said. 'Buck Grundy's wife was the only one lost. It always hits at night. The first thing that goes is the electricity, then the water comes in the door and windows. Well, Buck was alright but they found her body on Club Key, about ten miles back. Only reason they found her was the buzzards were circling.'

In the middle of a conversation he suddenly says, 'Fish.' Then you see the shadows coming out into the sandy arena. They appear in ones or twos, or little schools of five fish, 200 feet away. The sudden excitement has a bad effect on the casting, and this is the first opportunity I have had with the fly: tangling the line, whipping it, treading on it. It took two or three schools coming by to calm down and then even Bud couldn't understand why the fish weren't taking the lure. Often I was casting exactly to the right place. 'Come on, you snivelling coward,' he growled, then 'you dirty rat,' as the tarpon slipped away down the channel.

Leopard rays glided through the water – a nurse shark. Bud changed the fly, which looked almost identical to the last one. On the first cast, a tarpon swimming along the edge of the flat in a school of five, took it with a fierce snatch. My rod was high in the air, trying to strike, line floating around in the wind, but I didn't strip fast enough and he shook free. There was one other take, ten minutes later, but this time a moronic, hyperactive barracuda who had been lurking there all day chased the tarpon off the fly. And then suddenly they stopped swimming.

Hughes had craftily booked his guide for a further hour at nightfall, to fish the tarpon with lights on his last night. To be fair he asked me to come. He caught a 40lb tarpon on a jammed reel. I was, of course, pleased for him. He looked so *happy*.

1992

Learning to Live in Me-shaped Space

LAWRENCE NORFOLK

The engine noise drops and the air noise rises. Talking Dave shouts, 'Are you ready to skydive?' and Silent Dave climbs out to brace himself in the door. I shout, 'Ready!' and shuffle up to crouch sideways, one buttock balanced on the sill, legs dangling in the 70 m.p.h. slipstream. The altimeter on my wrist reads 12,000 feet. Talking Dave stares into my eyes to check that enough of my brain is working to get me down in one piece. He shouts, 'OK!' and Silent Dave shouts, 'OK!' Suddenly there is nothing much keeping me in this bucking speck of metal, except the fear I send down like radar to find the ground, and which the ground bounces right back up.

Everything down there on the ground has a bleached look about it – the haze, I suppose – and I'm rigid, grey-faced, sick. But I've trained for this, it's time to go, and 'down there' is so badly where I want to be right now that I do it. I jump.

Rituals and instruction. The drill. Some millions of years ago we crawled out of the slime and stood upright – but that's as far as we got, and fear of heights is the one terror we're all born with. We're wingless and stick-like. Basically unair-worthy. Just to get up there we need equipment. To get down we need technique, which is what we are here for – three students (Sam, Tony, me) with two instructors apiece on a decommissioned RAF bomber base at Langar outside Nottingham.

My instructors are both called Dave. Silent Dave (ex-King's Shropshire Light Infantry, 5,600 jumps) exudes calm, while Talking Dave (ex-packaging designer, 2,800 jumps) exudes confidence. Sam (a chocolate salesman) and Tony (horticul-tural lecturer) have both clocked up 40-odd static-line jumps. I have done absolutely nothing. On Day One, the combined freefall-jump scoreline reads: instructors 14,000–students 0.

We shout, 'LOOK-REACH-PULL!' and, 'LOOK-GRASP-PEEL-PUNCH!' We do dirt-dives and learn what a parachute can and cannot do. We jump out of a mock-up plane and 'ARCH!' and 'HARD ARCH!' We tear the cutaway pads and pull the handles on our practice-rigs. We simulate collapsed canopies and line-overs. We memorize the hand signals which our instructors will give us tomorrow in the air: Legs out! Legs up! Arms apart! ARCH! We learn about malfunctions because we want to jump, not fall, and we train like our lives depend on it because tomorrow, in part, they will.

Dawn: clear skies and a wind speed under fifteen knots means we jump. I don helmet, goggles, gloves, jumpsuit, altimeter. I check my rig. The little yellow handle at waist level on my right will deploy my main canopy. The Velcroed pad above will get rid of it. The metal handle on my chest pulls the reserve. Yellow, I tell myself. Think yellow. The Islander's engines start up. There's time for a last dirt-dive on the runway with the propellers blowing a realistic gale, then we climb aboard: three static-liners, John the cameraman, the Daves, and me. It's cramped, and hot, and I'm already sick with fright.

At 3,000 feet, Silent Dave throws out a piece of tissue paper weighted with plasticine. It's a marker to check the wind drift. It represents me at 12,000 feet. At 4,000 feet, the static-liners jump. Bam, bam, bam, gone. Just John and the Daves now. And me. Talking Dave asks me if I feel nervous. I nod. Silent Dave exudes calm, but not enough. I need oceans of calm, a whole skyful to unknot my muscles and keep the food from climbing out of my stomach.

At 9,000 feet, we run through what I'm going to do on the way down: pick a heading, check my alti, get hand signals, correct position, three practice pulls, check alti down to 5,000, then pull my yellow handle. That's what I'm going to do. Pull my yellow handle.

The check takes us to 11,000 feet, but this is where it gets bad. There's nothing to do but wait. I have to function, but my nerves are shot and there is absolutely nothing to do but nod, breathe and go grey. 'You're all there,' shouts Talking Dave above the engine noise. 'You're tense, but you're 100 per cent there.' I fight off fatalism, lassitude, the strong urge to give up. My mind might lock, my limbs freeze, and I need these things to get down.

I have never been this frightened before. 11,000 to 12,000 feet is absolutely the worst but, very weirdly, this helps. When the door opens, you can't take any more waiting and you can't take any more of the plane. You actually want to get out. Then the door opened, I went through the drill and I did get out.

The moments after exit are when you feel your speed the most. I threw myself out into nothing and the plane shot up like a rocket. Paradoxically, you are at your slowest, falling at maybe 50 feet per second by the time the shock at what you have just done recedes. The plane's slipstream carries you for a second or two, then you dive. Another two seconds and you are at terminal velocity (bad phrase), which is 200 feet per second. You are aware of your height only in an abstract way, but the air jams your senses in an instant. It's thinner up there, smells of nothing, and moves over your face at 120 m.p.h. There is no doubting that this is a wholly alien environment.

The Daves jump out with me, one each side holding me by the knees and elbows to get me in the right position. I feel stable. I shout 'Ground!' (my heading), turn my head and read the alti on my wrist, shout 'Eleven thousand feet!' These are my coordinates. I know, theoretically, where I am. Next come some practice pulls. Left arm over, right arm down. Everything has to be symmetrical in the air. On the ground you balance on something. Airborne, you balance *in* something and your smallest movement moves you. There are more dimensions, more ways to go unstable and generally fuck up. So you arch, and ARCH! and HARD ARCH! and you drop out of the sky, at 200 feet a second with your arms kinked out and yours toes pointed skywards. You look like a startled crab.

Your body doesn't know what else to do, so it pumps adrenalin. Sensory overload clears slowly. Your mind is almost completely taken up with a new and shocking idea: airborneness. Non-essential functions are jettisoned to make room for the important ones. There's no point listening to a 120 m.p.h. wind, so you don't hear it. Short-term memory also comes low on the list – I will remember very little of my first jump until several hours later. Body position, on the other hand, is vital. You feel your relative motions through the changes of air pressure on your limbs and respond microsecond to microsecond.

But absolute motion is done in the head. You have to *read* the ground, *read* your altimeter. You have to think, and all this through a blanket of fear, exhilaration, and another feeling that doesn't really have a name because human beings have never done this before. It's to do with the unnaturalness of it all, the sudden apprehension of something familiar as something alien. Being in what is usually up. Air weirdness.

I fell two miles in 50 seconds and dumped at 5,000 feet. I thought yellow handle, looked, reached, pulled. I counted to five and something jerked me out of the sky to leave me dangling under 300 glorious square feet of rip-stop porosity nylon. My Ram Air Canopy – enough lift to hold nineteen stones – had opened and would set me down light as a feather in five or six minutes' time. I looked around for the DZ and there it was dead ahead. I'd survived. I was fine. On top of the world. I didn't know it then, but I had just suffered my first malfunction.

There are mals, and then there are *mals*. A down draught at 50 feet can collapse your canopy and slap you into the ground in less than a second. A bad opening can snap your lines or, worse, wrap them around your legs. These are *mals*. I watched myself pull my yellow handle on John's video, saw the pilot chute and canopy bag fly up . . . And then fly down. There they were, bouncing around on my back as the down draught from two instructors and one blissfully ignorant student glued them to me. My parachute hadn't opened and I was plunging earthward. Then I saw Talking Dave reach over and slap the bag off, the pilot chute rise, and the bag spew the canopy over the sky. I was safe. But what if Dave hadn't been there to sort it out?

First, it wouldn't have happened – the down draught from two people flows between them, not directly on to someone's back (symmetry again). Secondly, I would have twisted and looked up to see what the hell was happening, a 120 m.p.h. wind would have shot past my armpit and knocked anything not firmly anchored to me up into the sky. Thirdly, I would have panicked, tumbled and got the same result. No doubt about it, this was a mal, and in the coming week I would get three more: two lots of twisted lines (solution: kick like hell until you unspin them) and a partially collapsed canopy, which I would only notice after three minutes of worse than usual steering (solution: pump the lines to get some *air* in there).

You jump out of an aircraft, and something goes wrong. It sounds terrible, but mals are frequent. They're preventable, or survivable, or both. Down draughts are caused by turbulence, which is caused by wind bowling over buildings and trees – so avoid buildings and trees. Line-overs are caused by pulling when unstable – so be stable, and if not then cutaway and go down on the reserve. There's time to think and act correctly. There are long seconds to save yourself. The air is blameless, and the ground is the ultimate known quantity. People die – and I will hear this repeated over and over – because they don't pull handles. The one way to certain death is simple: do nothing.

The Daves are unfazed by my mal. We debrief quickly and head up for the next jump. The plane experience gets worse, but the air experience gets better. I get stable quickly, go through my practice pulls and toe clicks and manage a wave to John's camera. I feel my brain start to clear and I grow aware that both the Daves have let go. I'm doing this on my own, and then, a second or two before dumping, I'm suddenly *there*. In it and part of it. Then my canopy yanks me up and the ground assumes its familiar nasty-carpet look. For a few brief seconds, I had it. Now I have to get it back. I steer my canopy down towards the DZ where, for me as for all skydivers, the flipside of this sport begins. *L'après-jump*.

The DZ is a place, and a state of mind. Four square miles of corn and grass bounded by trees (land away from), a road (avoid) and some power lines (AVOID!), is nailed by a control tower and crisscrossed by runways built long enough to get bomb-laden Lancasters airborne. A few extra-deep benches for kitted-up jumpers to sit in comfort with their rigs. The Cessna. The Islander. The packing mat. That's it.

The DZ is where you hang around before you jump, and when your jump is over, the DZ is where you are.

Static-liners, RAPS students, AFF students, the seasoned and the clueless, all mill about, practise their arches, stretch, yack, get their heads together, but most of all they wait. The DZ has an interim feel and the control tower is a hollow centre because the real focus of this place is two and a half miles above it. Up there. The air.

And that's where I'm starting to struggle, flailing, and my jumps are getting ragged. I'm forgetting signals, not checking my alti often enough. My head's all there, but my body is forgetting to do what I tell it, making slow right turns, de-arching and getting knocked about by the turbulence. To counter this last I am jumping with sixteen pounds of lead wrapped around me. Heat exhaustion joins the lengthening list of things I dislike about the plane (my nerves are getting better, but not much).

Talking Dave gets irritated. 'Legs out on exit, so slow right turn – *again*.' My head, my body, the air: we three are imperfectly connected. There's a me-shaped space up there where they meet and coincide – I know because I found it – and I'm close, but my outlines are off, my edges jagged. I'm not in it.

'Bitchin' skydive!' shouted Talking Dave after Jump Number Two, and Silent Dave murmured, 'Very enjoyable.' Now they are careful what they say around me, which discourages me further. When Mat (Asda Superstore shelf-packer, fourteen jumps) comes down hot and lands six feet from the Cessna, the bollocking he gets centres on the cost of the aircraft. It's code. The cost of a Cessna wing means Mat's potentially smashed legs. Talk of the propeller implies Mat being impaled on it. Mat's confidence needs adjustment, not wrecking, and it's the same with me, but in reverse. I'm tucking up, but I must not be told this. I feel patronized, then gloomy, then angry. 'Try and relax up there,' offers Talking Dave. 'Stop worrying,' adds Silent Dave.

Going up for Jump Number Five, I feel scared, hot, cramped – the usual – plus something else. It's puzzling, but I'm more than annoyed. Enraged. I'm scared every hour of the day, I'm not sleeping, every muscle in my body aches. I'm putting myself through hell and getting nowhere.

'Are you ready to skydive?' shouts Talking Dave. Fuck you, I think. Air noise, cloud, bad carpet, the first squirts of adrenalin, and then I jump.

Strictly speaking, the whole thing's a mess. I forget alti checks, flail a bit, and manage a miserable half-turn instead of the two full ones planned. But I remember pulling back my arms in a delta and shooting forward, feeling the air holding me smooth and steady, a cliff-face of cloud rocketing past on one side and me winging left to duck in under it, but most of all the sheer sense of being there. I leave the plane too angry to be scared, so I relax. Get into it. Somewhere in that jump I realize that the air has its substance and I have mine. We get along.

Gathering up my parachute some six minutes later, I know that Talking Dave will be shaking his head over the lousy exit and alti checks. But I also know that Jump Number Six will be near enough perfect, a good exit, alti checks, two full turns, a delta like a rocket and a pull smoother than silk. I'll be *there*. Back in me-shaped space. I'd found it again.

Me-shaped, you-shaped, he, she and it-shaped: there's room enough for all up there. Tall, short, fat or thin, the air will have a space for you. Find it, and you can skydive. The air is a harsh but democratic environment. It does not discriminate by race, creed, sex or colour. Or even experience. Five jumps or 5,000, what you are doing is in essence the same. Plunging, turning or tracking down, you are first among equals.

Hierarchies are for the ground, which, to skydivers, even the Sky Gods spiralling down on their zero-porosity handker-chiefs to strut their stuff on the packing mat, is only one of its many bad attributes.

Tall buildings, trees, telephone and power lines, fences, roads, down draughts, thorn bushes, water and nasty farmers are all features of the ground. If you are going to damage yourself, the ground is where you will do it. Locals taking a stand about engine noise have both feet planted firmly on (mired hopelessly in), what else, the ground. And, if you fall out of the sky at 120 m.p.h. and your mind freezes and you can't pull your handle, or you can and you panic and grab hold of your pilot chute and can't bring yourself to let go (as one jumper did), or you collide head to head with someone else and knock each other senseless (as two jumpers did), then the ground is where you will die.

I have my own problems with the ground on Jump Number Six. It comes up too slowly, or I flare too early. Whichever, I get a mouthful of grass. That apart, the jump goes as I knew it would – like a dream. I drill a tunnel through the cool stuff, carve arcs, open a curve and shoot forward over a sea of air. I turn to Dave and blow him a bye-bye kiss. I know I'm airworthy – most definitely back – then I find myself at 5,000 feet and pull. I'm gone.

Or, more prosaically, from Talking Dave's report in my log-book: 'Legs out again on exit and into right turn – corrected turn well. Stable at 11,000 feet then given thumbs up. Into track, but hands too close to the body and slow right turn. Good recovery then into good 360° left turn followed by good 360° right turn. Settled very well and holding heading, then turned round to face Dave. Good altitude awareness and clean solo pull at 5,000 feet. Well done!'

Or I'm *there*. Or I've got it. Or . . .

★

But got what? Where's '*there*'? And what the hell is 'me-shaped space'? What is this experience that gets people up there again and again?

Judd (signals engineer, 2,800 jumps) explains: 'Freedom. Megafreedom. Er . . . the breeze.' Alastair (police sergeant, 43 jumps) tells me he's tried to explain it to his friends. 'The gaps between my sentences just get longer and longer, then the gaps between the words. That's it, really. It's in the gaps between the words. In the silences . . .' John (cameraman, 2,000 jumps) looks gloomy and says, 'I've given up trying. I won't talk about it any more. I just won't.'

Groundlings see the sky much as skydivers see the ground – ambivalently. The stock response is rejection: 'I'd never do that,' or 'You must be mad.' At the same time our language is riddled with longing for this horrendous element. Walking on air, on top of the world, over the moon . . . When ground language needs hyperbole, it reaches for the sky. Or cries for the moon. Or jumps for joy . . . On the ground, these clichés are plasters to patch up Alastair's word-gaps, to fill in this experience that we dread, and want and cannot have. The air is where they come true.

Curiosity gets people up there, a deep breath and some bottle gets them through the terror. But skydiving is what you find beyond the curiosity and terror. If it's an emotion, it's not one found anywhere on the ground. It's a mode of being without precedent, and that, essentially, is the attraction. You get this nowhere but up there and that's what drags you back. Most of all when it's rushing towards you at 200 feet per second, the ground (and all that goes with it) may as well not exist.

Skydiving is not *like* anything else. Anything else is not like *it*. That's why those people are up there, and that's the problem with explaining it. Between the air and the ground there is absolutely no relation; ground-based terms of reference don't apply. Whether learning to skydive, surviving it, enjoying it, describing it, or explaining it, the ground is no help at all.

So I'm with John: I just won't. And with Alastair, because I can't. And with Judd, who gets to the heart of the matter at the second attempt: 'It's just different. It's totally different. You can't really explain to a person what it's like. You just have to do it yourself.' I'm with the air addicts and jump junkies, the Sky Gods and DZ bums, airboys and airgirls, who are either up there doing it, or down here waiting to, for whom there is no explanation, only the imperatives: Get up there. Do it. Jump.

1992

Jimmy White and his Magic Finger

LAURA THOMPSON

'It was the most incredible shot I've ever seen,' said my father, who has played a lot of snooker in his time. 'He had to get out of a snooker, an impossible snooker. The cue ball was touching this other ball. He had to get away from it, come right round it and hit the brown. He sat on the edge of the table. He had his cue up here – *vertical* – and he hit away from this other ball, and the cue ball made the shape of a horseshoe, came round and hit the brown. The ball did a U-turn. It was quite unbelievable.'

'Massé shot, I remember it,' says Jimmy White. 'It is a difficult shot, yes. But I was about 50 in front and so I went for it. If it had been closer, in a big competition, I would have tried to find another way of getting out of the snooker. Of course, years ago, I'd have attempted the massé without even thinking about it.'

I can remember when he would have done that: when Jimmy White was the whirlwind, an unstoppable, unruly force scoring sky-high breaks and hardly ever winning tournaments. 'When he came on the scene, when he was only a boy – we're going back more than ten years now – I'd never seen anything like him, the way he could pot balls,' said my father. 'He had this cue action – it was like he had a long finger that he was putting on the table and pointing at the balls. No doubt about it, he was the best player of them all, the best *natural* player. But when I used to watch him – well, he made me go hot and cold, the way he carried on.'

'Yes, all I used to do was pot balls,' says White. 'I had no position or nothing. It took me about ten years to get that out of my system, because I just loved potting balls. To play a safety shot was like turning the game off. I was like a frustrated boy with his Tonka toy – I wanted to be playing all the time. "This is *my* shot," you know.'

Now, however, it seems that the days are gone when the young Jimmy White rammed balls as if he were firing bullets and hang the bloody aftermath. 'It was very hard at first, to tighten myself up. I wasn't getting a lot of pleasure out of it at all. But once you start getting the results . . . I still go for my shots, I haven't completely lost that instinct, to go for what I see, but I try not to give it to 'em on a plate any more – I make 'em work for it. I got sick of losing, really.'

Last year was Jimmy White's most successful yet – he won the British and European Opens, the Rothmans Grand Prix and the UK Championship – so it is clear that the more careful game he has been developing since around 1990 is paying dividends. His whole life has become more careful of late. He is 31 this year, with a wife and four daughters, and the years of throwing money at bookmakers and disappearing on three-day benders are, so he says, also gone. The whirlwind has calmed itself. He has become a rich man, a Mercedes driver, a golf player. And he has traded in some of the pure love that he had for snooker, the pure pleasure that he got from the touch of his long, sure finger, for some of the success that his pure ability merits. Perhaps that is what the most naturally gifted sportsmen have to do – subsume the lawless individualism of their talent into the disciplined, unforgiving, wider world of the game.

Yet, somehow, one feels that even if Jimmy White were to play like Steve Davis for the rest of his life, he would still be regarded as a man at the mercy of his own exquisite, unbiddable talent. Those who love him – and they are many – yearn for him to win. They were thrilled when he finally learned how to play safe, because they too were getting sick of him losing: but they never really *believe* that he is going to win. They believe that he will always and for ever cause them to sway from bliss to agony with his deathless pots and his imbecile misses. They never really believe that the spring Bank Holiday spent in front of the green baize altar, praying for the Easter Monday ascension of Jimmy White, will find its fulfilment in the moment when he is finally crowned World Champion of snooker. They want that moment, though, almost as much as Jimmy White himself wants it. They know that if – *when* – it comes, it will seem as if they are sharing it with him. That is how he makes them feel.

My attitude to snooker is very simple – I can't be bothered to watch it when Jimmy White isn't playing and I can't bear to watch it when he is. I want him to win too badly. For the last three years I have sat behind the chinks in my fingers, waiting for his victory in the World Championship, but not really believing that it will come. Defeat in the 1990 final was bearable because Stephen Hendry played like a demon child and because, well, there would always be another chance. In 1991, it seemed that maybe that chance had come. John Parrott? Ha! I prepared myself for Jim's moment of glorious triumph even as Parrott, rising with bland-faced efficiency to the occasion, won the first seven frames of the final without missing a ball.

'I can appreciate what he did, yeah, looking back. Sad that it happened to me, but . . . It's like in any sport, though. If you can't accept it when someone plays very well, then deep down you're not really a player.'

Then, in 1992, Jimmy got a third chance. Parrott was out, Hendry was out of form. 'This is Jim's year,' said my father. 'Ah, don't say it yet,' said my mother. I watched the final at my parents' house and every time Jimmy won a frame, we punched the air and whooped like gamblers watching a 25/1 horse cross the winning line. Every time he missed a ball, we tossed and muttered as if suffering from a terrible seasickness.

Eventually, however, it seemed to me that Jimmy, at 14 frames to 8, was so far ahead of Hendry he could not possibly be caught. I went upstairs for some new air and prepared myself for the moment of glorious triumph. I could hear the rhythmic clock-cluck of the balls and the punctual applause of the crowd, but just as these noises were slipping into my subconscious, I began to discern another series of sounds as well. 'Oh Jim,' my mother was saying. 'Oh Jim, Jim.' 'You silly bugger!' my father was saying. 'Jim, you silly bugger.'

I ran back downstairs as if I'd overheard a declaration of war. 'What's happened?' I said. Jimmy was sitting in his chair, a sad dandy, face quenched yet flushed, lower lip tucked away like a bewildered six-year-old's, mournful London eyes like those of a betting shop manager's mongrel. 'I'm going to bed,' said my mother. 'I can't worry any more, he's worn me out.' 'The boy's catching him hand over fist,' said my father despairingly. 'Jim's bottle's gone.'

This subsidiary talent of Jimmy White's, this ability to lay bare the nerves of those who love him, to tune them taut as guitar strings, to play upon them those bravura flourishes, those twanging discords, is of course as appealing to his followers as his primary talent. He creates such *drama* when he plays snooker, drama as intense and claustrophobic and unrelenting as a production of *Miss Julie* staged in a pub theatre during a heatwave. It is even more dramatic than when Alex Higgins used to bustle round the table burning up energy, the ground, the table, fags, time, life, because Alex was never *loved* in the way that Jim is loved. Watching Jimmy White is unbearable, but people relish the misery. They were certainly relishing it down in Newport, where I met him during the Welsh Open tournament, when he was 4–0 up against Dene O'Kane and needed only one frame to win.

It should have been, could have been, so easy. Coming back into the hall after the interval, I believed that Jimmy would simply win the frame and have done with it; momentarily I had forgotten what he is like. Now I watched as shots of bold delicacy were accomplished while journeyman pots were muffed. To the ecstatic exasperation of the crowd, he managed, by working at it, to lose the next two frames and was on the verge of losing a third when O'Kane, bending at last to the collective will, miscued on an easy black and Jim padded up, on his rippling, unfolding feet, to clear the table. It was then that I noticed the felicity with which the snooker balls that he pots tumble into the pockets, as if his long finger has guided them there with a certain *tendresse*. Now his earlier remark to me, that he 'fell in love with snooker', no longer seemed a banality but the simple truth.

Judging by the reaction to even this minor victory, it makes no difference where Jimmy White plays; always, following him around, will be the note of barely contained mob hysteria, heard in the wild whoops of triumph, the breaking surges of love that grow to meet the moment when he pots the final black.

My father: 'Jim is arguably the most popular sportsman in the country. I've never, ever met anyone who didn't want him to win.' A gut connection ties together Jimmy White and the people who watch him. He sits bravely blinking as defeat whirls around him and you are right there with him. He smooths down the black silk fluff of his hair before taking hold of a trophy and you are right there with him. He may not be liked by as many people as the Mansells, the Faldos, the Christies, but he seems not to be disliked by *anybody*, which is not something one could say about the others. His achievements may not compare with theirs, but something about the way in which they are performed touches the collective heart of the public. There is something innocent, something vulnerable, something generous, something staunch, something completely removed from self-glorification or analysis.

One possible definition of a sporting hero is that he is a man who does what you do, who lives your life – but better. Jimmy White embodies this definition more fully than any other sportsman I can think of. Only his phenomenal ability separates him from the people who love him. Nothing else.

Snooker players *en masse* do seem to have a closer connection with their public than most sportsmen. There are exceptions, but on the whole they are very accessible, strolling around, mingling among the people to whom they are hero-mates. Because they don't have to be fit, they are free of that slightly precious, puritanical quality harboured by more athletic types, and, of course, they are free to drink. Most sportsmen, when one meets them, are very highly defined, as if they have a black line drawn around them, but snooker players are fuzzier. They look like men one might meet in a pub: which explains why other men feel relaxed and friendly towards them and why women feel that it is safe and reasonable to fancy them.

With Jimmy White, people seem to feel acutely this appearance of accessibility. They feel that they know him. 'Is he like he seems to be?' they said to me, after I had interviewed him. 'Ah, yes, I thought he would be.' My father questioned me about him, and to every single thing I said he replied: 'Well, I knew he'd be like that. I could have told you that without you going to meet him.' In a way, he was right. Jimmy White was exactly what I expected him to be. His image is what he is like and his image is what he is. Sitting in his loosened black waistcoat like an off-duty Sam Weller, chatting amicably in his small, sweet, toothy, Tooting voice, he is viscerally relaxed, unthinkingly himself. A working-class English everyman with a long, magic finger.

In fact, if his image *were* manufactured, then people would scarcely believe it, it is so much of a piece. It is as if a bad journalist with streetwise pretensions had decided to try his hand at a Channel 4 screenplay about the life of a snooker player: 'A "wide boy" with a heart of gold, "Jimmy" is raised in the terraced anonymity of south London . . .' The perfection of the image is that it is all true. Jimmy White really did play truant from school and hide from the authorities in a snooker hall. He really did go hustling with Tony Meo and blow all the money that he won on horses, dogs, cards – 'But that's all behind me now. Well, I have a bet on the snooker, but I don't back myself any more.' He really did meet his wife in a chip shop when he was fifteen. He really did leave school scarcely able to read and write. He really hasn't ever had a job other than that of snooker player.

And he really does seem not to have been changed by the acquisition of fame and money. He may have Ron Wood watching him in the audience at tournaments, but likely as not Ron will be sitting next to Jimmy's father. His heart is warmed by the prospect of returning to practise at the same club, the recently re-opened Zan's in Tooting – 'It's been shut for years, I can't believe it, it's really brilliant' – where he first played almost 20 years ago.

'I only went in there because when it was raining we couldn't go on the common and things like that. I never played at all. And then one day I had a few shots. And that was it, I fell in love. But it took about two years before I could play at all – my highest break for two years was 25.'

However, when he was fourteen, his headmaster saw him play in a charity match and was so impressed that he struck an agreement with him to curb his truancy: that he need attend school for only half of each day, spending the other half in the snooker club. 'And I thank him now. Mr Beattie, his name was.' Whether Mr Beattie knew what White was doing in his half days off and whether, had he known, he would have been quite so liberal in his attitude, one cannot say.

'Tony Meo and me, what we used to do, we'd put our money together and just get a tube map out, or a railway map, put our finger somewhere – say it'd be Bedford, somewhere like that – and go to the place. And in them days, the late Seventies, there was a lot of snooker halls. You'd have clubs where within an hour the locals would get their best player in to play you. And then me and Tony would play him, win his money, and be off home and somewhere else the next day.

'We never left 'em unhappy. We was gone before they realized they'd been hustled . . . No, but we didn't actually *hustle*, really – we didn't play bad and then someone would have a bet and we'd play well. We used to go straight in there and declare to them that we were there to win.'

I asked him if snooker is more boring for him now. 'No. But the atmosphere in the clubs, in them days, was incredible. They were like a base to . . . I don't know, to get away.

'I don't get bored with playing. There's millions of shots in snooker. The travelling is the only hassle, but I can't knock it, because once I'm there playing, I'm in my element.'

For all his appearance of accessibility, there is something impenetrable about Jimmy White. The self-conscious games that are played by most famous people – by most *people* – are designed to conceal, but in fact they reveal. Jimmy's openness and naturalness are so total that he becomes, conversely, enigmatic. Beneath his guise of the working-class English everyman, one feels that the most important thing about him is the thing that differentiates him from everyone else: the long, magic finger, the love and talent that he has for snooker.

He has no fake modesty about it. He knows just how good he is and he knows, too, that as the most naturally gifted player of his generation, it would be wrong if, somehow, the World Championship were to elude him. Those who love him are waiting for their collective heart to crack with sentiment, for the London roar to be unleashed, as he pots the final, victorious black; he is surely waiting for that wrong to right itself. Why, yearning for him to win as I am, do I feel him to be at the mercy of his exquisite, unbiddable talent, as if a gift of that kind comes at a price? Why is this the thrilling, uneasy sensation that I get when I watch him play?

The man himself is more robust. He has, after all, over the last couple of years, trimmed the excesses of his talent to suit the demands of the game. He has, perhaps, shown it who is boss. 'Now I just feel it's in my own hands. Without being flash, you know.'

1993

Playing Handball with Zeus

TIMOTHY O'GRADY

A friend of mine was driving through the Cabrini Green housing project towards downtown Chicago on an autumn afternoon in 1991. Cabrini Green is notorious for its violence and deprivation in a city that knows much of both. While he was waiting for the traffic lights to change, the car in front of him suddenly pulled over to the pavement. A tall shaven-headed man wearing sunglasses, gold jewellery and an expensive suit got out of the car and trotted across an area of wasteground to an open basketball court where a group of boys were playing ball. Everything stopped when the man arrived, the ball rolling across the court in the sudden silence. The man picked up the ball and hit a long jump shot through the rusted rim. The boys stood in place, frozen, slack-jawed, because, my friend now realized, the man in the suit was Michael Jordan, the highest-paid athlete in the world and perhaps the greatest basketball player of all time.

What happened then? I asked him.

'They played basketball.'

What was it like?

'It was the 20 minutes of a lifetime. If you were an Italian peasant it would be like the blessed Virgin appearing to you. In ancient Greece it would be like playing handball with Zeus.'

★

When I was the age of the boys playing basketball, Zeus to me was Arnold Palmer. Whether he won or lost, and how he did it, had an urgency and importance that I did not feel again until I watched Muhammad Ali box in the 1970s. Palmer was the active agent in an alchemical formula whose other ingredients were television, a golf-playing President in the White House and the immediate sense of unfettered possibility that characterized the 1960s.

In the game of cool strategists, Palmer was like a tag-team wrestler. Gary Player said that when he first saw him hitting balls, sparks seemed to fly up from the grass. He lunged at the ball with such force that he often lost his balance. His face in its emotiveness was like violently changing weather patterns. He was often to be seen deep in a wood, grass and twigs flying up around him, his club waving before him and his torso bobbing like a middleweight's as he strained to follow the flight of the ball through an improbably tiny aperture in the branches of a tree up ahead. Everyone watching him looked as anxious and expectant as he did, as though all their assets would be frozen if the shot failed. His golf was always a spectacle of the possible, however remote, rather than the probable. There was a drama even in the way he stood over the ball, because no one had any idea what would happen next. 'Arnold would never protect a lead,' said Lee Trevino. 'He'd just keep firing for birdies. He'd go for the flag off an alligator's back.'

This may go some way towards suggesting why he so quickly wore out the word 'charisma' for golf journalists. Jack Nicklaus said that all Arnold Palmer had to do was put on his glove and hitch up his trousers and everyone would ooh and aah. Trevino thinks he 'has more charisma taking the clubs out of the back of his car than the rest of us do walking up the eighteenth fairway winning a major championship'. People seemed to feel that their fates were bound up in his.

I had followed Palmer around during the 1960s in his practice rounds for the Western Open. The idea then of actually playing golf with him was the sort of idle notion boys entertain themselves with before going to sleep. Like punching out the local thug. Or being marooned somewhere with Brigitte Bardot. Or shooting baskets with Michael Jordan. Twenty-five years later I wondered if such an idea could somehow be brought to life and, as it happened, just before New Year's Eve and after fifteen months of letters and phone calls, I got word from Pennsylvania that, if I still wanted a game of golf with Mr Palmer, I was to be at the first tee of the Bay Hill Club in Orlando, Florida at 12.20 p.m. on January 12.

I arrived three days early with a bad back and nearly nauseous with nerves. Arnold Palmer's name and face were everywhere, because he is the owner of Bay Hill – Palmer winning the Masters; Palmer and Jack Nicklaus; Palmer and a couple of presidents; even Palmer and Michael Jordan – 'To my legend of golf, looking forward to playing a game with you one day, Michael Jordan.' I had never been in a place like it before – millionaires' villas lining fairways; an immaculately manicured championship golf course; bellboys, shoe polishers, club cleaners, maids, caddies, starters, waiters, assistant pros and barmen all calling you by name within a half-hour of arrival.

I hit some balls at the range, small dull shocks skittling around the base of my spine, and then introduced myself to Jim Deaton, the head professional. I asked him if he could tell me what it was like to play golf with Arnold Palmer. 'The first time I played with Mr Palmer,' he said, 'I couldn't feel my thumbs for the first eleven holes. I hardly said anything at all because I kept rehearsing everything in my mind before I said it so I'd get it right.'

The next day I played a round with two chiropractors

from Michigan. As we came off the first green one of them pointed over to a small, fenced-in area at the back end of the driving range and said, 'Isn't that . . . him?' And there he was, the king of golf, prowling around a putting green on his own like a bear in a cage. The tension ratcheted up another notch.

The following night, around midnight, I lay on the floor of my room to do some exercises prescribed by the chiropractors. I heard an irregular series of faint clicks outside and I went on to the balcony to have a look. The day had been cloudy, but a huge V-shaped fissure had opened in the sky to reveal a full moon and a knee-high white mist clinging to the base of the palm trees and drifting gently along the ground. On the practice green, four teenage boys were having a putting contest. They looked almost incorporeal in the moonlight and mist.

Just beyond them was the first tee. What was to happen to me there the next day at 12.20? Would I move the ball sideways three yards back through my legs? Would the driver fly out of my hands? The father of a friend of mine was once invited to an outing at a club he had never played at before and, on the first tee before a crowd of waiting golfers, had swung and missed twice. On his third attempt the ball dribbled forward 20 yards to the front of the tee. He then turned to his gallery, solemnly shook his head and said, 'Tough course.' At least I would have a line in the event of disaster.

Arnold Palmer passed into legend in the summer of 1960 at the Cherry Hills Golf Club in Denver, Colorado during the final round of the US Open. The first hole at Cherry Hills is a tight, downhill 346-yard par four guarded by trees on the left, a ditch on the right and a strip of heavy rough across the centre of the fairway 50 yards from the green. Almost everyone in the tournament played the hole with a one iron and a wedge in the hope of a birdie. Palmer believed he could eagle the hole by driving the green. In the first round he had a six, in the second a five, and the third a four, losing between three and six shots on a hole that, played conservatively, was yielding many threes. At the end of the third round Palmer found himself in fifteenth place, seven shots behind the leader, Mike Souchak. Between them were, among others, Ben Hogan, Sam Snead and Jack Nicklaus.

As he was having lunch before teeing off for the final round, a journalist stopped at his table. 'I suppose you'll be using your one iron on the first hole today,' he said.

Palmer looked up from his food. 'I'll be using my driver,' he said.

'What's the point?' said the journalist. 'Go for pars. You'll be in the money.'

Palmer now looked at the journalist as though the man had insulted his mother. 'What if I shoot 65?' he asked.

'Arnold, forget about it,' said the journalist. 'Only one man in the history of the US Open has ever shot 65 in the final round. You're out of this tournament.'

'If I shoot 65, that will give me a total of 280,' said Palmer. '280 usually wins the US Open.'

The journalist rolled his eyes and proceeded on his way. Palmer, fuming, swallowed down the last of his lunch, went out to the first tee, took out his driver and creased the ball high up into the mountain air and on to the green 346 yards away. He took two putts for a birdie. He then birdied the second, third, fourth, sixth and seventh — six birdies in the first seven holes. He went to the turn in 30, finished, as he said he would, with a 65, and won the Open championship.

What made him a legend was not that he'd won a major tournament, or even that he had done so in such a spectacular way, but that he had played with such publicly evident hunger and emotion. American professional golfers tend to arrive at adulthood with a sensibility not unlike that of nuns. They generally display their talent and therefore their vocation early, get tracked on to junior golf programmes, play on intensively coached college teams, go through the PGA qualifying school and then join the tour. Their training has concentrated entirely on technique and strategy. Their devotion is singular and methodical, like prayer. Because they are so rarely at home, their lives become purged of personal continuity. Many are emotionally neutered.

Palmer followed this path until the autumn of 1950. His father was a pro and he began playing when he was three years old. He was one of the great college players of his time. It was all but inconceivable that he would not turn pro. Then his closest friend and fellow golfer Buddy Worsham was killed in a car crash on his way back from a dance. Palmer was nearly paralysed with grief. The future he had been moving inexorably towards vanished. He accompanied his friend's body back to his family in Washington, DC and tried to continue his life, but couldn't. 'I didn't know what to do with myself,' he said. 'I stayed in school until I thought I'd go crazy – every time I'd turn around to tell him something I'd realize he was gone for ever.' He then dropped out of school and signed up for three years in the Coast Guard.

When he emerged from this exile in 1954 he won the US Amateur, got married and turned pro. He quickly became characterized by charging putts at the hole from 50 feet and beyond and crashing his driver off the fairway to water-encircled greens 280 yards away. His swing was a wild, ungainly, muscular explosion that almost no one could understand. Tony Penna, a leading pro at the time, passed Palmer on the practice range and said to a friend, 'I hope that guy hasn't given up his day job.' After he played a practice round at Augusta before the 1958 Masters with Ben Hogan and two other pros, he overheard Hogan asking one of them in the locker room, 'Tell me, what is that guy Palmer *doing* here?' Palmer went on to win the tournament, his first major.

The emotion with which he played could also produce the spectacle of a fall – as at the 1961 Masters when he took a six at the eighteenth to lose by a shot, or the 1966 US Open, when he dissipated a seven-shot lead with only nine holes to play and lost in a play-off to Billy Casper, a catastrophe that sent many Americans into mourning for the rest of the summer. But he utterly dominated golf for the first half of the 1960s. He won scores of tournaments, compiled what is still the best record in the Ryder Cup and over one six-year stretch won seven out of the 25 major tournaments he entered. No one felt safe, even with a five-shot lead on the last day, with Palmer coming up behind them.

This incredible dominance ended with the emergence of a force that no one could have predicted – Jack Nicklaus. Theirs became one of the great rivalries in the history of sport, one which Palmer says 'is still as fierce as ever'.

At 12.10 the starter announced through a loudspeaker: 'First group of the shoot-out to the tee, please – Mr Palmer, Mr Dameron, Mr Mitchell, Mr Dorman and Mr O'Grady.' Palmer came down the steps from the pro shop, put on a straw hat and walked over to the tee. So did players coming off the ninth and eighteenth greens, everyone from the practice putting green, several from the driving range, caddies, club attendants, assistant pros and a number of people in the middle of their lunch.

All four of my playing partners hit good, long drives into the heart of the fairway. Palmer's ball took off from the face of his large, metal-headed driver as if out of the mouth of a cannon and sailed off into the atmosphere beyond the range of my eyesight. I was last. My chest felt like it was in flames. Gary, my caddy for the day, handed me my driver. I bent over to tee the ball up, looked along the ground, and there, just a few feet away, was Arnold Palmer. I could see his white Nike shoes, his sharply creased blue trousers, the powerful, veined forearms and blacksmith's hands, the fingers round and surprisingly short, like chipolatas. When I interviewed José Maria Olazabal he told me that on the first hole of his first professional tournament his hands were shaking so badly he could not get the ball to stay on the tee. This now began to happen to me, the ball clattering on the tee like teeth in a cold wind. Above me, as if from the clouds, I heard Palmer speak. 'Take it easy,' he said, so quietly that no one else could have heard. 'We're just here for an afternoon of golf. Enjoy yourself.'

I stood up, swung back, and the ball came off the centre of the club, up over a tree that guarded the slight dogleg, and settled down on the left side of the fairway, seventeen yards behind Arnold Palmer's.

I watched his back as he strode up the first fairway of his own golf course. The man who created the modern game by drawing into it millions of dollars in sponsorship is, at 63, still the fourth-highest earning athlete in the world. No living golfer earns more than he does. Much of the money he earns from golf comes from the design and management of courses as widely dispersed as Italy, France, Japan, Taiwan, China and Morocco, as well as all over the United States. He still earns the equivalent of several people's annual incomes from competition alone, and two weeks after I played with him he beat Jack Nicklaus, Raymond Floyd and Chi Chi Rodriguez in a skins game, taking home $190,000. But even the eight or nine million he earns every year from golf is dwarfed by the hundreds of millions in annual turnover generated through property, corporate and other business interests which include Sears, Rolex, Penns Oil, Fuji Electric and the sponsorship of Japanese bedlinen. He not only flies his own plane, but runs the fixed base operation for private jets in Chicago. He was until recently the largest Ford dealer in the world.

He had found $30 along with the rest of us to throw into the pot for the shoot-out competition that day. Our fivesome comprised a team playing against several others in a game in which the best three scores on each hole counted, the winning team taking all the money at the end of the day. Handicaps did not count. I held some useful pars on the third, fourth and sixth, but I three-putted the par three second after a good shot to the green, threw two other pars away through indifferent chipping and left a birdie putt on the lip at the seventh. I hit an eight iron second to five feet at the tenth, but misread the birdie putt and then missed a four-footer for par at the twelfth. 'Damn,' said Arnold. 'I was counting on you to make that.' I slunk slope-shouldered from the green, like Bernhard Langer after missing the putt that would have held the Ryder Cup.

He was playing with at least two full sets of clubs and six putters, one set of irons just off the forge and the other bandaged with strips of lead tape. He experimented ceaselessly. On the eleventh he left the metal driver in the bag and hit a very new-looking club with a persimmon head. The ball floated a bit, a few degrees off to the right and shorter than usual. He lifted the club up to his nose, stared at it and declared, 'You're retired.' I hit my drive slightly off the toe, but as it drew in it seemed to catch a slipstream of air that kept it afloat. As I watched it fall I heard him say, 'Tim, if you've outdriven me, that club is going into a coffin.' I was at least fifteen yards behind him.

I had thought until I played at Bay Hill that I could hit the ball a reasonable distance. Billy Dameron, a retired businessman, was regularly 20 yards past me off the tee, with Palmer 20 yards further than that. On par threes where I was hitting a three iron, Palmer would use a six. He is tremendously powerful through the arms and shoulders and still exudes a physical well-being and athleticism. Standing over the ball he is as strong and solid as a Doric column.

From what I had read, the source of his physical strength, as well as his character and style of playing golf, seemed to have been his late father, the head professional at Latrobe Country Club in western Pennsylvania, a coal and steel mining area otherwise famous for producing football players: Joe Namath, Mike Ditka, Dan Marino and Joe Montana all come from there. 'My father was one of the strongest men I ever met,' he told me. 'He could do ten pull-ups with either arm and go practically all day if he used both. He was a severe disciplinarian and a great man for manners, but above all he had respect for other people. He told me that if I wanted to go to sleep with a clear conscience I should treat everyone I came across as if I myself were that person. I would remember this when people would wave their tournament programmes at me to sign. He instilled in me how important it is to take people as they come and to care about them. Because of the way he raised me I don't think there was any chance of me going off the rails or acting like a big shot, but if I had he would have been there to make me see sense. For a long time I didn't even think he believed I could play golf. I had won the US Amateur, a lot of pro tournaments and two Masters before he even congratulated me. It was after the US Open at Cherry Hills and he said, "Nice going, boy." I thought the world had come to an end.'

By the time we came to the sixteenth, a par five, we were three over par as a team and the jackpot had probably slid away. But Arnold was still going for birdies. He hit a two iron second over the water and on to the fringe of the green. His ball had settled down into some thick grass and when he half-fluffed his chip he winced as though a knife had been slipped up under his ribs. 'If I could play that shot I'd have won four more US Opens,' he said to the sky. He then holed his ten-foot putt for a birdie four.

His driving is very long and probably more accurate than when he was at his best. He holed a lot of putts and his iron shots all seemed to fly straight out of the heart of the club. Above all, he seemed to hit the ball with a sense of relish and adventurousness in a way that other people go hang-gliding. What, then, was the difference between his game now and when he was at his best?

'The main thing missing now is what has been missing for the past twenty years – concentration. The concentration used to be just automatic. I was always completely in the game. Concentration comes out of a combination of confidence and hunger. One year when I was still in college I entered the Azalea Open, which was a professional tournament down in North Carolina. I stayed with some friends of mine who had a cottage there and while we were having a few beers around the table the night before the tournament one of them asked me what I was going to do the next day. I said, "I'll tell you what I'm going to do," and I went through the entire eighteen holes, shot by shot. Then when I went to bed I dreamed it all over again, the whole round of golf. And when I played the next day I did exactly what I said I would. I shot 65.'

Didn't you get a little nervous around the fourteenth? I asked him. Weren't you afraid that you might wake up?

'No. I was *loving* it. It was the same with the last round at Cherry Hills. But then you become a victim of yourself. It's like a big home-run hitter who hits sixty home runs one season and then next spring, when he's looking at the pitcher, he's thinking, "Damn, I've got to hit sixty home runs this season." He tries to protect what he's done, and the doubts come in, and maybe that year he only hits ten home runs. In golf you know you can play the game but you begin to think, "I've got to keep the ball in the fairway," or "I can't afford to three-put." Where you used to attack, now you're protecting. It all just gets fed into the diet and you find you're not winning tournaments like you used to do. Whether you win again at all depends on how well you handle this. But nobody escapes it. It's like death. If you hang around long enough it's going to get you.'

I had another competition going on in my mind that day apart from the shoot-out. It was match play, me against Arnold Palmer, him playing off scratch and me off my handicap of twelve. The match was not at all viable because Palmer did not know about it. Probably if he had he would have turned his attention towards it and annihilated me. But as it was, I was three up going into the last three holes. I lost the sixteenth with a par to his birdie. I fell to pieces on the par three seventeenth, hitting two balls in succession into the water. One up with one to play. I would have to win or draw the last for there to be a conclusion, because there could be no play-off for a game that did not exist.

The eighteenth is one of the best and toughest finishing holes on the pro tour. From the back tee it is 441 yards to a green protected in front and around the right by a lake and everywhere else by bunkers. It was here that Robert Gamez hit a dramatic seven iron second into the hole to win the Nestlé Invitational from Greg Norman, a shot commemorated by a plaque on the fairway. From the regular tee about 20 yards closer to the hole I hit a high, rather weak drive into the right rough, the worst side from which to approach the green. Arnold hit a tremendous drive into the centre of the fairway precisely to the 150-yard mark. I had about 210 yards, all carry, over the lake to the green. The ball was sitting up well and I thought I could fade a four wood over the edge of the lake and then up the length of the green. I hit

it well, but it didn't fade. It flew up over the lake, hit beyond
the pin at a narrow part of the green and then ran up a little
incline between two bunkers. Arnold turned around from his
position 60 yards in front of me and treated me to a little
round of applause. He then called to Billy Dameron, 'Can I
get there with an eight iron?' Billy nodded. He then hit what
looked like a great shot. I thought it was all over the pin. But
it hung in the heavy air, came down on the far bank of the
lake and skidded back into the rocks. From there he took a
one-stroke penalty, chipped up to a foot and got the putt for
a five, and a one over par 73 for the round. I had a downhill
lie, with the green running away from me downhill to the
water. If I hit it at all thin, that is where the ball would wind
up. I asked Gary how he thought I should play it. He handed
me a sand wedge and told me to float the ball very softly to
the fringe in front of the bunker on my left and let it run
down to the hole. I looked at the ball the way you'd look
into the eyes of a lover just about to leave by train for
Istanbul. The ball went up as though buoyed on a little cloud.
'Man, that ball is in the hole,' said Gary, but it caught some
thick grass on the fringe and rolled only a few feet on to the
green. But I got the twelve-foot putt for a par. Two up on
Arnold Palmer – in my imaginary match play.

Afterwards we had a few beers in the locker room. I asked
him who had the best golf swing he had ever seen. 'Snead,'
he said. 'It was the most fluid, the most natural, the most . . .
authentic.' Authentic is an unusual word to attribute to a golf
swing, and perhaps also to legends. Legends often have, if not
a regal disdain, then at least an inviolable assumption of
status. They can be distrustful, even paranoid, about the
attentions of others. Their minds can wander in the presence
of those who have not accomplished what they have. Some
perhaps try to confirm who they are by making those around

them nervous. But Arnold Palmer seemed to me to have obliged his father's wishes. He is generous and solicitous in his attention. On his way to the locker room he talked for nearly a quarter of an hour to two boys who asked him for his autograph. There seemed to be nothing staged or consciously directed about this. He is at ease with himself and has the gift of putting others at their ease, as I had found on the first tee. He is fluid, natural and authentic.

Before I left I asked him what he thought his greatest strength as a player had been. Year after year, golf magazines judged him the best long iron player in the game. He was renowned for his power, his attacking play, his ability to escape from trouble and his fearless putting. He didn't pause before answering.

'Desire,' he said.

1993

The Education of Mike Tyson

PETE HAMILL

An artificial Christmas tree stands in a corner of the waiting room, with a bunched-up bedsheet at its base feigning snow. Unmatched pieces of cheap furniture, some wicker, some plastic, are arranged awkwardly around the edges of the room. It could be the antiseptic lobby of a second-class motel except for the view through the picture windows behind the Christmas tree: two parallel steel-mesh fences topped with barbed wire and a slope of sour lawn rising toward blank walls and tan-brick buildings. The complex is called the Indiana Youth Center. But it's not a place where schoolkids play checkers or basketball on frigid afternoons. The barbed wire makes it clear that this is a jail.

So does the posted rule against bringing drugs or alcohol on visits; so does the order to place wallets and handbags in a locker in the far corner, along with all cash in excess of five dollars, any pens, notebooks, tape recorders, books, all hats and overcoats; and so does the stamping of your hand with invisible ink, the emptying of pockets into a plastic tray, the body search, the passage through a metal detector.

The rules of entrance obeyed, I walk down a long, wide ramp into the prison, pause at a sign forbidding weapons beyond this point, and wait for a steel-rimmed glass door to be opened. Up ahead there are other such doors, with guards and a few prisoners moving languidly along a corridor that is lit like an aquarium. The door in front of me pops open with a click. I turn right to a guard's booth, where I hand over my pass and am told to thrust my right hand into a hole in a wooden box. An ultraviolet light certifies the stamp. I am then instructed to go through the door to the left, into the visitors' lounge, and give the pass to the guard behind the high desk in the corner. I do what I am told and wait. In the lounge a dozen couples sit facing each other on thick plastic-covered chairs, maintaining space and privacy, drinking soda bought from machines, trying hard to be loose, glancing tensely at the clock, conscious of time. Behind them a wall of picture windows opens upon a vista of grey grass and blank, tan walls. The Indiana sky is the colour of steel.

Then, suddenly, from another door, Mike Tyson appears. He smiles, gives me a hug, and says, 'How are ya, buddy?'

Twenty-two months have passed since he vanished from the nightsides of cities, from the bubble of champagne and the musk of women, from the gyms where he prepared for his violent trade, from the arenas that roared when he came after an opponent in a ferocious rush, his eyes hooded, gleaming with bad intentions. Twenty-two months have passed since he was convicted of raping an eighteen-year-old beauty-pageant contestant who consented to leave her own Indianapolis hotel room at nearly 1.30 in the morning, who moved around the streets for a while with Tyson in his rented limousine, who then went to Tyson's suite in the Canterbury Hotel, where she sat on the bed with him, went to the bathroom and removed her panty shield, on the way passing the door that led to the corridor and the possibility of flight. Twenty-two months since the jury believed Desiree Washington lay helpless while Tyson had sex with her. Twenty-two months since the jury believed that it was perfectly normal for a rape victim to spend two more days taking part in the

Miss Black America pageant of 1991. Twenty-two months since Michael Gerard Tyson, twenty-five-year-old child of Amboy Street, Brownsville, Brooklyn, was led away – refusing to express remorse for a crime he insists he didn't commit – deprived of his freedom, his ability to earn millions, his pride.

But if there is anger in him or a sense of humiliation, neither is visible on this grey morning. He is wearing jeans and a white T-shirt – with his prison number, 922335, hand-lettered over his heart – and to a visitor who first met him when he was sixteen, he looks taller somehow. In the TV-news clip that plays every time his name is mentioned, Tyson weighs about 250 pounds, swollen and suety in a tight-fitting suit as he smiles in an ironic way and holds up his cuffed hands on his way to a cell. Now, a few days before his second Christmas in prison, he is about 220, the belly as flat as a table, the arms as hard as stone. He looks capable of punching a hole in a prison wall.

'Yeah, I'm in good shape,' he says, 'but not boxing shape.' He works out in the prison gym every day, a self-imposed regimen of calisthenics, weights, running. 'No boxing,' he says, the familiar whispery voice darkened by a hint of regret. 'They don't allow boxing in prison in Indiana.' He smiles, nodding his head. 'That's the rules. Ya gotta obey the rules.'

We walk over to the chairs, and Tyson sits with his back to the picture windows. His hair is cropped tight, and he's wearing a moustache and trimmed beard that emphasize the lean look. Then I notice the tattoos. On his left bicep, outlined in blue against Tyson's ochre-coloured skin, is the bespectacled face of Arthur Ashe, and above it is the title of that splendid man's book *Days of Grace*. On his right bicep is a tattooed portrait of Mao Tse-tung, with the name MAO underneath it, in cartoony 'Chinese' lettering. I tell Tyson that it's unlikely that any other of the planet's six billion inhabitants are adorned with *that* combination of tattoos. He laughs, the familiar gold-capped tooth gleaming. He rubs the tattoos fondly with his huge hands.

'I love reading about Mao,' he says. 'Especially about the Long March and what they went through. I mean, they came into a village one time and all the trees were white, and Mao wanted to know what happened, and they told him the people were so hungry they ate the bark right off the trees! What they went *through*. I mean, *that* was adversity. This . . .'

He waves a hand airily around the visiting room but never finishes the sentence; he certainly feels that the Indiana Youth Center can't be compared to the Long March. I don't have to ask him about Arthur Ashe. For weeks Tyson and I have been talking by telephone, and he has spoken several times about Ashe's book.

'I never knew him,' Tyson said one night. 'I never liked him. He was a *tennis* player, know what I mean? And he looked like a black bourgeois, someone I couldn't have nothin' to do with. Just looking at him I said, "*Yaaagh*, he's *weak*." That was my way of thinking back then.' A pause. 'But then Spike Lee sent me his book, and I started reading it, and in there I read this: "AIDS isn't the heaviest burden I have had to bear . . . being black is the greatest burden I've had to bear . . . Race has always been my biggest burden . . . Even now it continues to feel like an extra weight tied around me." It was like *wham!* An extra *weight* tied around me! I mean, wow, that really *got* me, and I kept reading, excited on every page.'

On the telephone, with the great metallic racket of prison in the background, or here in the visiting room of the Indiana Youth Center, Tyson makes it clear that he doesn't want to talk much about the past. He doesn't encourage sentimental evocations of the days when, as a raw teenager from a reform school, he learned his trade from the old trainer Cus D'Amato in the gym above the police station in Catskill, New York.

He doesn't want to talk about his relationship with Don King, the flamboyant promoter whose slithery influence many blamed for Tyson's decline as a fighter and calamitous fall from grace. He is uncomfortable and embarrassed discussing his lost friends and squandered millions. He has no interest in retailing the details of the case, like another Lenny Bruce, endlessly rehashing what happened on July 19, 1991, in room 606 of the Canterbury Hotel or the astonishingly feeble defence offered by his high-priced lawyers or his chances for a new trial. He wants to talk about what he is doing now, and what he is doing is time.

History is filled with tales of men who used prison to educate themselves. Cervantes began *Don Quixote* in a Spanish prison, and Pancho Villa read that book, slowly and painfully, while caged in the Santiago Tlaltelolco prison in Mexico City more than three hundred years later. In this dreadful century, thousands have discovered that nobody can imprison the mind. In the end, Solzhenitsyn triumphed over Stalin's gulags, Antonio Gramsci over Mussolini's jails, Malcolm X over the joints of Massachusetts. From Primo Levi to Václav Havel, books, the mind, the imagination, have offered consolation, insight, even hope to men cast into dungeons. I don't mean to compare Mike Tyson to such men or the Indiana Youth Center to the gulags; Tyson is not serving his six-year sentence for his ideas. But he understands the opportunity offered by doing time and has chosen to seize the day.

'Sometime in that first month here,' he said one night, 'I met an old con, and he pointed at all the guys playing ball or exercising, and he said to me, "You see them guys? If that's all they do when they're in here, they'll go out and mess up and come right back." He said to me, "You want to make this worth something? Go to the library. Read books. Work your mind. Start with the Constitution." And I knew he was right.'

And so Tyson embarked on an astonishing campaign of exuberant and eclectic self-education. Early on he read George Jackson's prison classic, *Soledad Brother*, 'and the guy knocked me out. It was like any good book: the guy sounded like he was talking directly to me. I could *hear* him, I can hear him *now*. He made me understand a lot about the way black men end up in prison, but he didn't feel *sorry* for himself. That's what I liked. I got so caught up with this guy, he became a part of my life.'

Tyson has been reading black history too. He is fascinated by the revolution in Haiti in the early nineteenth century, 'the only *really* successful slave revolt, because blacks took *power*'. He can quote from John Quincy Adams's defence of the slaves who mutinied on the Spanish ship *Amistad* in 1839 off the coast of Cuba and sailed for fifty-five days all the way to New York. 'They landed in Long Island,' he says. 'Imagine! Long *Island*.'

The process of self-education did not begin smoothly. In his first weeks in jail, Tyson enrolled in a school programme, then quickly dropped out. 'You know, I'm out on the streets, I'm out there, or I'm training, or I'm in the bars, I'm chasing these women. Then I come to this place after not going to school since I was what? Sixteen? Seventeen? They hit me with this thing, they said, "Bang! Do this, do this work . . ." It was like putting a preliminary fighter in with a world champion.'

Dispirited, angry at the teachers and himself, he dropped out for a while. 'Then I started very gradually studying on my own, preparing for these things. Then I took that literacy test – and blew it out of the water.'

He went back to classes, studying to take a high school equivalency examination and met a visiting teacher from Indianapolis named Muhammad Siddeeq.

'He was just talking to the other kids one day and said,

"Does anybody need any help? If so, I'll help you in the school process." And I said, "Yeah, I need help." So he showed me things, in a simple way . . .'

One thing Tyson learned quickly was the use of percentages and decimals. 'I never learned that before,' he says, still excited. 'It's a small thing, maybe, something I shoulda learned in grammar school. But you come from a scrambled family, you're running between the streets and school, missing days, fucking up, and you end up with these *holes*. One thing never connects to another, and you don't know why. You don't know what you didn't learn. Like percentages. I just never learned it, it was one of the holes. I mean, later on I knew what a percentage was, you know, from a $10 million purse, but I didn't know how to do it myself. That was always the job of *someone else*.' He laughs. 'One thing now, I can figure out how to leave a tip. There's restaurants out there where I should eat for free for a couple of years.'

He isn't simply filling those gaping holes in his education that should have been bricked up in grammar school. He reads constantly, hungrily, voraciously. One day it could be a book on pigeons, which he raised with great knowledge and affection in the Victorian house where he lived with D'Amato and D'Amato's longtime companion, Camille Ewald, whom Tyson calls 'my mother'. But on other days he could be reading into the history of organized crime, thrilled to discover that the old Jewish gangsters of Murder Inc. hung out near Georgia and Livonia avenues in Brownsville, walking distance from his own childhood turf. He discovered that Al Capone was from Brooklyn and went west to Chicago. And there were black gangsters too.

He talks about Lucky Luciano, Meyer Lansky, Bugsy Siegel, Frank Costello – some of the Founding Fathers of the Mob – with the same intensity and passion he gave as a teenage fighter to Ray Robinson, Mickey Walker, and Roberto

Duran. The old gangster he's most impressed by is the gambler Arnold Rothstein. 'He was smart – Damon Runyon called him the Brain – and figured out everything without ever picking up a gun. He helped teach these younger guys, like Lansky and Luciano, you know, how to act, how to dress, how to behave. In *The Great Gatsby* – you know, by this guy F. Scott Fitzgerald? – the gambler called Meyer Wolfshiem, he's based on Arnold Rothstein. I mean, this guy was *big*.'

In one way, of course, studying such histories is a consolation; in a country where the percentage of young black males in prisons is way out of proportion to their numbers in the general population, it must be a relief to learn that the Irish, Italians and Jews once filled similar cells. But Tyson's study of organized crime is part of a larger project.

'I want to find out how things *really* work. Not everything is in the history books, you know.' A pause. 'Some of those guys didn't like blacks. They sold drugs to blacks. They poisoned black history. They didn't respect us as human beings. But most of them couldn't read and write. The first ones came to this country ignorant, out of school, making money. They didn't have any kind of morals. They wanted to be big shots and they wanted to be respected by decent people. They tried to be gentlemen, and that was their downfall. When you try to be more than what you really are you always get screwed up.'

He emphasizes that gangsters are not heroes. 'You can read about people without wanting to be like them,' he says. 'I can read about Hitler, for example, and not want to be like him, right? But you gotta *know* about him. You gotta know what you're talking about. You gotta know what *other* people are talking about before you can have any kind of intelligent discussion or argument.'

So it isn't just gangsters or pigeons that are crowding

Tyson's mind. He has been poring over Niccolò Machiavelli. 'He wrote about the world we live in. The way it really is, without all the bullshit. Not just in *The Prince*, but in *The Art of War, Discourses* . . . He saw how important it was to find out what someone's motivation was. "What do they want?" he says. What do they *want*, man?'

And Voltaire. 'I loved *Candide*. That was also about the world and how you start out one thing and end up another, 'cause the world don't let you do the right thing most of the time. And Voltaire himself, he was something, man. He wasn't *afraid*. They kept putting him in jail, and he kept writing the truth.'

He has recently read *The Count of Monte Cristo* by Alexandre Dumas, aware that the grandmother of the French writer was a black woman from Haiti. 'I identify with that book,' he says. 'With Edmond Dantès in the Château d'If. He was unjustly imprisoned, too. And he gets educated in prison by this Italian priest.' He laughs out loud. 'And he gets his *revenge* too. I understand that; I feel that. Don't get me wrong, I don't want revenge against any person. I don't mean that. I mean against fate, bad luck, whatever you want to call it.'

He is familiar with the Hemingway myth that so exhilarated earlier generations of Americans: Hemingway the warrior, Hemingway the hard drinker, Hemingway the boxer. But he talks most passionately about Hemingway the *writer*. 'He uses those short, hard words, just like hooks and uppercuts inside. You always know what he's saying, 'cause he says it very clearly. But a guy like Francis Bacon, hey, the sentences just go on and on and *on* . . .'

Obviously, Tyson is not reading literature for simple entertainment, as a diversion from the tedium of prison routine. He is making connections between books and writers, noting distinctions about style and ideas, measuring the content of books against his life as he knows it. But he is not taking a formal course in literature, so I asked him one night how he made the choices about what he reads.

'Sometimes it's just the books that come to me. People send them and I read them. But sometimes, most of the time, I'm looking. For example, I'm reading this thing about Hemingway and he says he doesn't ever want to fight ten rounds with Tolstoy. So I say, "Hey, I better check out this guy Tolstoy!" I did, too. It was *hard*. I sat there with the dictionary beside me, looking up words. But I like him. I don't like his writing that much because it's so complicated, but I just like the guy's way of thinking.'

Along with literature, Tyson has been reading biographies: Mao, Karl Marx, Genghis Khan, Hernán Cortés. In casual talk, he scatters references to Hannibal, Alexander the Great, Oliver Cromwell. 'When you read about these individuals, regardless of whether they're good or bad, they contribute to us a different way of thinking. But no one can really label them good or bad. Who actually knows the definition of good or bad? Good and bad might have a different definition to me than it may have in *Webster's Dictionary*, than it may have to you.'

He knows that for *his* life, the models in books might not always apply. But in all such books, he insists that he finds something of value.

'I was reading Maya Angelou,' he said one evening, 'and she said something that equates with me so much. People always say how great a writer she is, and people used to say to me, "Mike, you're great, you could beat anybody, you don't even have to train." But you know how hard it is for me to do that? To win in ninety-one seconds? Do you know what it takes away from me? And Maya Angelou said about herself it takes so much from me to write, takes a lot out of me. In order for me to do that, she says, to perform at that level, it takes everything. It takes my personality. It takes my creativity as an individual. It takes away my social life. It takes away *so much*. And when she said that, I said, "Holy moley, this person understands me." They don't understand why a person can go crazy, when you're totally normal and you're involved in a situation that takes all of your normal qualities away. It takes away all your sane qualities.'

In prison Mike Tyson is discovering the many roads back to sanity.

One of those roads is called Islam. Tyson was raised a Catholic by his mother, Lorna, and during the upheaval in that time before he went to jail, he was baptized as a favour to Don King in a much-photographed ceremony presided over by Jesse Jackson. But water, prayer and photographs didn't make him a born-again Christian. 'That wasn't real,' he says now. 'As soon as I got baptized, I got one of the girls in the choir and went to a hotel room or my place or something.'

Now he has embraced Islam. In a vague way, he'd known about Islam for years; you could not grow up in the era of Muhammad Ali and know nothing about it. 'But I was avoiding it because people would press it on me. I always avoided what people pressed on me. They wanted me to do the right thing – and Islam, I believe, is the right thing – but all these people wanted me to do the right thing for the wrong reason.'

In prison, through his teacher, Muhammad Siddeeq, Tyson started more slowly, reading on his own about the religion, asking questions. He insists that Siddeeq is not a newer version of Cus D'Amato. 'He's just a good man,' he says, 'and a good teacher.' Nor does Tyson sound like a man who is making a convenient choice as a means of surviving in jail. He admits that 'there are guys who become Muslims in jail to

feel safe – and give it up the day they hit the streets again.'
Tyson might do the same. But in repeated conversations, he
sounded as if he'd found in Islam another means of filling
some of those holes.

'I believe in Islam,' he told me one night. 'That's true. It's
given me a great deal of understanding. And the Koran gives
me insight into the world, and the belief of a man who
believes that God has given him the right to speak his word,
the prophet Muhammad, peace be unto him. I look at Islam
from different perspectives, just as I look at everything else. I
find it so beautiful because in Islam you have to tolerate *every*
religion, you know what I mean? 'Cause everyone has different beliefs. Most so-called religious leaders are bullshit. Voltaire knew that, knew organized religion was a scam. Their
object is power. They want power.'

Tyson's scepticism about organized religion includes some
of the sects and factions within Islam. He pledges his allegiance
to none of them.

'One guy says, "I believe in Islam, I live out of the Koran."
Well, I believe in *that* but *other* than that, please . . . They got
a sect here and a sect there. Unbelievable. I just don't understand that. How can *I* be a Muslim and *you* be a Muslim, but
we have two different beliefs?'

Tyson thinks of Islam as not simply a religion but a kind of
discipline. He says he prays five times a day. The Koran is a
daily part of his reading (but obviously not the only reading
he does). 'And you know, I got a sailor's mouth,' he laughs.
'But I've cut down my cursing at least 50 per cent.' He clearly
needs to believe in something larger than himself, but his
choice of Islam is entwined with a revulsion against certain
aspects of Christianity.

'If you're a Christian,' he says, 'and somebody's a Christian
longer than you, they can dictate to you about your life. You
know, *this* is what you should do, and if you don't do *this*,

you're excommunicated. I just found that bizarre ... in conflict with human qualities, you know what I mean? I couldn't understand why a person couldn't be a human and have problems and just be dealt with and helped. In Islam there's nobody who can put you in your place. They can let you know this is wrong, you need help on this. But the only one that can judge you is Allah.'

I asked Tyson how he could reconcile his embrace of Islam with the fact that many of the slave traders were Muslims. The horrors of the Middle Passage often began with men who said they accepted Allah. Tyson answered in a cool way.

'Look, everyone in Arabia was a slave, know what I mean? They had white slaves, black slaves, Arab slaves, Muslim slaves. Everybody there was a slave. But the slave traders were contradicting Islam and the beliefs of Islam. The prophet Muhammad, he wasn't a slave trader or a slave. As a matter of fact, the Arabs were trying to kill him, to enslave him. People were people. But Europeans took slavery to a totally different level. Brutalized, submissive, abhorrent. But you can't condemn all the Jews or all the Romans because they crucified Christ, can you?'

Tyson emphasizes one thing: he's a neophyte in his understanding of Islam and has much to learn.

'Being a Muslim,' Tyson says, 'is probably not going to make me an angel in heaven, but it's going to make me a better person. In Islam we're not supposed to compete. Muslims only compete for righteousness. I know I'm probably at the back of the line. But I know I'll be a better person when I get out than I was when I came in.'

For the moment, jail is the great reality of Tyson's life. Unless a court orders a new trial or overturns his conviction, he will remain in prison until the spring of 1995. The Indiana Youth Center is a medium- to high-security facility and looks relatively tame compared with some of the others I've seen in New York and California. Boredom is the great enemy. 'I get up and eat and go to class,' he says, explaining that he doesn't eat in the prison dining room, because 'the food is *aaaccch*' but goes to a commissary where he can buy packaged milk, cereals, and other food, paying from a drawing account called the Book. He works out in the gym every day, shadowboxing, doing push-ups, running laps to keep his legs strong and lithe. 'There's nothing else to do,' he says. 'You gotta keep busy so you don't go crazy.'

But it's still prison. For now it's the place where Mike Tyson is doing time, using all of his self-discipline to get through it alive.

'I'm never on nobody's bad side,' he says. 'Even though there's guys in here just don't like the way you walk, the way you look, or whatever, I just – I'm never on nobody's bad side. I don't like to be judgmental, because we're all in the same boat. I have to remember to be humble. But sometimes I get caught up with who I was at one time, and I must remind myself my circumstances have changed.'

There are still a lot of hard cases on the premises, including Klansmen and members of the Aryan Brotherhood. Tyson laughs about their swastikas, shaved heads, white-power tattoos. 'They talk back and forth,' he said. 'But they realize once they're in prison, no one gives a fuck about them.'

More dangerous are people who seem to crack under the stress of doing time. 'A couple of days ago, this guy who never bothered nobody just cracked a guy on the head with a lock in his sock,' he said in an amazed tone. 'And there are other guys – they'll do something disrespectful to some guy, and they'll walk around with their headphones on, acting like they didn't do anything, jamming, dancing, then, next thing you know – *ka-pow!* – they get clocked.'

In the bad old days, Tyson might have empathized with

such people; he is, after all, the man who as champion once socked an off-duty heavyweight named Mitch Green in Harlem at 4.00 in the morning. But in prison, he is at once part of the general population and detached from it because of his celebrity. 'When I get out, I have a future,' he says. 'A lot of these guys don't.' Sometimes he even volunteers for a form of solitary confinement ('to be alone, to focus, to meditate, to read, *to get some fucking sleep*'). But he also looks with compassion on his fellow prisoners.

'They send some guys to prison that don't necessarily have bad records,' he says. 'Instead of rehabilitating him, they *de*habilitate him by sending him to prison. Without him even being attacked or molested, just from what he witnesses, some things that are so taboo to his humanity. It could totally drive him insane.'

Among the scarier aspects of prison these days is AIDS. 'They are falling like flies in here,' Tyson said. 'And some of these guys keep boning each other over in the dorms.' There are other people for whom prison is life itself. 'There's one guy here who's been inside for thirty-one years. Not in *here* but in other prisons. There are other guys with so much time . . . I watch them adapt. This is their home. You don't go in their door without knocking.'

Tyson said that much of what he has seen is sad and comic at the same time.

'You see a guy, he's doing all the time in a lifetime, he's talking to a girl on a phone. I mean, he's doing *ninety years*. And what's he saying? "Don't go out tonight, baby. Don't go out tonight, baby. Don't go out tonight, baby."'

Tyson laughed in a sad, rueful way.

'Most guys that are in here, they got a lot of time, so they lose hope. They get caught up in the sideshows, like homosexuality, drugs, you know what I mean? It's very difficult for me to think about participating in the things these guys do. You talk to the guys, and to me they seem rather sane. But to see their conduct, some of them, they're in a totally insane frame of mind. The fact is, prison is like a slave plantation. We have no rights which the authorities respect. I wasn't a criminal when I got put in here. I didn't commit no crime. But we become the problem *out there*, because we're not aware. We become the problem because out there we're robbing, we're stealing, we're selling drugs, we're killing. I hear people talk about revolution. They mention Castro, Mao, Lenin, the Black Panthers. But how can you have a revolution when you have crime, when you have people selling drugs, you have people murdering? There's no collective ideas there.'

I asked Tyson if the young prisoners from Indiana resembled the young men from his Brooklyn neighbourhood. He said that many of them did. When he was champion, Tyson refused to offer himself as a role model; he certainly doesn't see himself as one now. But he does understand the Brownsvilles of America.

'At the age of ten or fifteen, you become very influenced by what you see,' he said. 'You see these guys looking good, with fly cars, nice girls on their arms. You think this is what you want to be. But any kind of proper success has to do with education, unless you're an athlete, and everyone's not going to be Michael Jordan or Muhammad Ali. You fall in bad company. You see drug dealers and gangsters with all their bullshit. You know *they* didn't go to school. So you don't fill the *holes*. You go after the wrong shit. The thing I've noticed in here, with the white kids and the black kids and the Latin kids and the Asian kids – the only thing they have in common is poverty.'

I asked him if drugs were another common factor. Tyson himself was never a druggie in the conventional sense; his drugs were liquor and celebrity. He whispered, 'Of course.'

'Drugs and women,' he said. 'You know, we all run through the same complexities in life.'

Among those many complexities in American life is racism.

'It's very difficult being black,' he said one evening. 'These reporters came to interview me from South Africa, and one of them asked me was I racist. And I said, "Yes, I am a racist – to people who are racist toward me." I never liked to believe that I'm a racist because of the way I was brought up, both from my mother and from Cus and Camille. But, you know what I mean, sometimes things are in the air and people say or do things detrimental or hurtful towards you. You strike back at them. That's what I meant in that interview. Not *all* white people. Shit, no. *Those* people. Those specific people. I just want to be treated the way I treat people.'

Behind many of these feelings are jagged memories of that Brownsville childhood. 'Too many guys, too many black people, men and women, *hate* themselves. They see the shit around them and they give up before they ever start. They get one or two little tastes of power – sticking a gun in somebody's face – and then it's over.'

He was in jail when the riots erupted in Los Angeles, and he hated what he saw on CNN.

'It could have all been prevented if people believed in fairness and equality. But you have to understand: the things that people do and what they *should* do are totally different. We should live like every man is equal, every woman is equal. But how we *do* live is, You get yours, I get mine, fuck you.' He talked about Rodney King. 'Some guys in here, they heard Rodney King and they laughed. But what he said was powerful, man. Why *can't* we live together? Why the *fuck* can't we all live together?'

In jail Mike Tyson is engaged in an admirable attempt to find out who he is, to discover and shape the man who exists behind the surface of fame and notoriety. There is no Cus to explain the world, to tell him what to do. In the end, there's only himself. And because he is in prison, this is no easy process.

'You have good days, and you have bad days, but you just think to yourself, *This isn't the end.* You say, "I was kind of wild out there; maybe I was heading for something more drastic." Which is all a part of playing head games so you won't get insane.'

Like anyone in prison, Tyson misses life on the outside. He misses certain people, and in most of our talks he circles back to Cus D'Amato. 'A lot of things Cus told me, they are happening now,' he says. 'But at that time, I didn't keep them in mind, because I was just a kid. Cus tried to store everything in my mind so fast. He didn't think that he was gonna be around. He tried to pack everything in at one moment, you know what I mean? I'm trying to be a fighter, I'm trying to have some fun on the side, and I'm just running crazy. Now I think about him all the time. Like, damn! Cus told me that. And God! He told me *this* too. And, oh! He told me that.

'He was always saying to me, before I was anything: "What are you gonna do? Look how you talk to me *now*," he said. "Look how you act. How you gonna act when you're a *big-time fighter*? You're just gonna dump me." I said, "I'm not gonna do that, Cus. I'm not gonna do it." And I didn't.' He laughs. 'I used to say, "Cus, I'll sell my soul to be a great fighter." And he said, "Be careful what you wish for, 'cause you might get it."

'I miss him still. I miss him. I think about him. No, I don't dream about him; I don't dream much in this place. But I miss Cus. I still take care of him, make sure nothing bad happens, 'cause I promised Cus before he died to take care of Camille. I was young, I was, like, eighteen, and I said, "I can't

PETE HAMILL

fight if you're not around, Cus." And he said, "You better fight, 'cause if you don't fight, I'm gonna come back and haunt you."'

The ghost of Cus D'Amato doesn't haunt Tyson; if anything, the old manager instilled in the young man a respect for knowledge and a demand for discipline that are only now being fully developed. 'Cus had flaws, like any man,' Tyson says. 'But he was right most of the time. One thing I remember most clearly that he said: "Your brain is a muscle like any other; if you don't use it, it gets soft and flabby."'

Other things do haunt Tyson. One of them is that fatal trip to Indianapolis. 'I had a dick problem,' he admits. 'I didn't even want to go to Indianapolis. But I went. I'm in town with the best girl [rapper B Angie B] that everybody wants. And I had to get this – why'd I have to do that, huh, man? Why'd I have to do that? I had a girl *with* me. Why'd I have to make that call? Why'd I have to let her come to my room?'

He has his regrets too, and says that he is trying hard to acquire some measure of humility, leaning on the Koran.

'Remember, when I accomplished all that I did, I was just a kid,' he says quietly. 'I was just a kid doing all that crazy stuff. I wanted to be like the old-time fighters, like Harry Greb or Mickey Walker, who would drink *and* fight. But a lot of the things I did I'm so embarrassed about,' he said. 'It was very wrong and disrespectful for me to dehumanize my opponents by saying the things I said. If you could quote me, say that anything I ever said to any fighters that *they* remember – like making Tyrell Biggs cry like a girl, like putting a guy's nose into his brain, like making Razor Ruddock my girlfriend – I'm deeply sorry. I will appreciate their forgiveness.'

He isn't just embarrassed by the words he said to fighters. 'I have girls that wrote to me and said they met me in a club,' he says. 'And I said something crazy to them. And I *know* I said that, you know, 'cause that was my style. And I say, wow, what was going through my *mind* to say that? I don't dwell on it too much. But I just think: *What the* hell *was I thinking*? To say this to another human being?'

Tyson tries to live in the present tense of jail, containing his longing for freedom through a sustained act of will. But when I pressed him one evening, he admitted that he does yearn for certain aspects of the outside world.

'I miss the very simple things,' he said. 'I miss a woman sexually. But more important, I miss the pleasure of being in a woman's presence. To speak to a woman in private and discuss things. Not just Oh! Oh! Oh! More subtle than that. I just want to be able to have privacy, where no one can say, "Time, Tyson! Let's go!" You miss being with people. I miss flying my birds. They're not gonna know me, I'm not gonna know them, 'cause there're so many new ones now 'cause of the babies. I miss being able to hang out. Talk to Camille. Laugh. I miss long drives. Sometimes I used to just get in the car and drive to Washington. I miss that a lot. I miss, sometimes, going to Brooklyn in the middle of the night, pulling up in front of the projects and one of my friends will be there, shooting baskets. I'll get out of the car, and we'll talk there, like from 4.00 in the morning until 9.00 or 10.00. People are going to work, and we're just talking.' A pause. 'I miss that.'

He insists that he doesn't miss what he calls the craziness. 'It was all unreal. Want to go to Paris? Want to fly to Russia? Sure. Why not? Let me have two of those and three of them and five of those. Nobody knows what it's like — fame, millions — unless they went through it. It was unreal, unreal. I had a thousand women, the best champagne, the fanciest hotels, the fanciest cars, the greatest meals — and it got me here.'

He does have some specific plans for the future. 'I want to

visit all the great cities, I want to see the great *libraries*,' he says. 'One of the few things I did that impressed me was going to Paris that time and visiting the Louvre. I was *devastated* by that place, man. I want to see all of that, everywhere.'

Yes, he said, he will box again. He will be twenty-eight when he returns, the same age as Ali when he made his comeback and certainly younger than George Foreman when he made his. He asks repeatedly about active fighters and how they looked in their latest bouts, because he only sees brief clips on CNN. 'I'm a fighter,' he says. 'That's what I do. I was born to do that.'

He wants to make money; nobody knows how much Tyson has left, not even Tyson, but his return to boxing could be the most lucrative campaign in the history of sport. 'I want to have money for a family,' he says. 'In the end, that's how you can decide what kind of man I was. Not by how many guys I knocked out. But by the way I took care of my kids, how I made sure they went to college, that they had good lives and never wanted for nothing. And what I taught them. About the world. About character.'

Tyson would even like to try college himself. 'I'd like to go to a black college that's not well-known,' he says, 'to study and learn. But also to have some kind of exhibitions, too, fights to benefit the college. I don't have to fight benefits for a church or a mosque. But the black colleges, *that* I want to do . . .'

In the end, of course, all education is self-education, and Tyson is clearly deep into the process. The faculty of Tyson's university includes Cus D'Amato and Alexandre Dumas, Machiavelli and the prophet Muhammad, Dutch Schultz and Ernest Hemingway, and dozens of others. Part of the curriculum includes what some academics call life experience. There are millions of college graduates who don't know what Tyson knows. About writers and thinkers. About life itself.